COMPELLED

HOW TO LIVE FOR SOMETHING BEYOND YOURSELF

DR. SURESH KUMAR

Published in the United States by Harvest India Media.
www.harvestindia.org

Library of Congress Control Number: 2014949285

ISBN-13: 978-0-692-27638-9

Printed in the United States of America

Design and layout by 8TRACKstudios
www.8TRACKstudios.com

Cover photos by David Trotter

I dedicate this book,
first to the glory of God,
and to my dear mother, Lalitha Kumari,
who never gave up on me and
introduced me to the Lord Jesus Christ.

To my dear wife, Heny Christina, my son David,
and my daughters Mercy and Nancy,
who have given me the freedom
to father the fatherless
and put the Kingdom of God
before their own needs.

Preparing for ministry at Bible College

CONTENTS

"I'm so glad that Suresh, President of Harvest India, finally wrote a book. Compelled illustrates what it looks like to really live a life of faith and believe that God is going to do something miraculous. This book will challenge the way you live your life everyday for Christ."

Brad Lomenick
Former president and key visionary - Catalyst
Author - "The Catalyst Leader"

FOREWORD

Nine years ago, I experienced India for the first time with a team of pastors. We rode through busy city streets and walked through humble villages with wide-eyed wonder. There seemed to be a collision of beauty and brokenness on display at every glance.

The desperation of these people was vast and overwhelming. Yet hope was also clearly on the rise. We encountered Christian men and women with unquenchable resolve to live out the Gospel in their nation in the most compelling and tangible ways. The leader of these leaders was Suresh Kumar.

It has been the privilege of our church, **ROCK**HARBOR, to partner with Suresh through the work of Harvest India for almost two decades. We have seen countless lives redeemed and futures changed. We have watched orphans, lepers and prostitutes be welcomed to new homes, new families, new worth. Thousands who were furthest from Jesus have been raised up to carry His name as church planters and world changers. And, in truth, our work together has just begun.

Yet for me, perhaps the greater privilege has been to call this courageous visionary a trusted friend. Just a month ago, Suresh and his wife Christina sat across from me in my church office offering much needed counsel. As Suresh heard my heart and spoke into my wrestlings, I was struck by the paradox of this man. Many times I have seen him preach before multitudes with unrivaled passion and power. But in this quiet conversation, his words were just as weighty. Suresh is a man who speaks, and writes, with authority that has been tested by a life of deep faith and perseverance.

This rare, lived-out authority flows onto the pages of "Compelled". Each chapter provokes questions, stirs inspiration, and lays new foundations for a compelling life of faith. Given the endless stream of books and blogs that so mark Western Christianity, I believe we can sometimes drown in a sea of good spiritual advice. Yet in the thick of many clever ideas, strategies and perspectives, there is the occasional voice that breaks through - and rings true with clarity and conviction.

COMPELLED

Suresh Kumar is a voice worth listening to, and without question, a leader worth following. As he unpacks his story through "Compelled", we are challenged to consider and reclaim our own. In echo of Paul's call in 1 Corinthians 11:1, Suresh has written a bold invitation to "follow my example, as I follow the example of Christ." And for all who dare to follow Jesus, one of the greatest gifts we can receive is someone to show us the way.

Do not read these words as more tips to a better life.
Dive in – all in – to discover the life you were created,
saved and empowered to live.

Todd Proctor - Lead Pastor
ROCKHARBOR Church
Costa Mesa, California
August 2014

INTRODUCTION

HOW TO USE THIS BOOK AS A GROUP STUDY

Although you are welcome to read COMPELLED on your own, there is something transformational about reading and discussing it together within your small group, Bible study, or Sunday school class. At the end of each chapter, I have included study questions in three categories...

- **Getting Started** - re-connect and break the ice with your group.
- **Going Deeper** - dig into the key ideas and Scriptures.
- **Applying It To Your Life** - make a plan to take action.

You don't need to be a Bible scholar to lead a group - simply someone who can facilitate a discussion based on what you've read.

Simple Instructions

1. Read the chapter during the week.
2. Write out your answers to the study questions in the book.
3. Come to your group prepared to discuss what you're learning.

I believe God will do something powerful in your life in the weeks to come! Let's get started...

CHAPTER 1

WHAT IS COMPELLING YOU?

Once again, I find myself sitting in the passenger seat bouncing along a winding, dirt road. With a car in front of us and a van behind, we're kicking up clouds of dust that eventually float over the heads of workers in the rice paddy on our right.

The sun is shining with all its might, and the humidity hangs like a thick, invisible fog in the air. With our windows rolled down, the gust against our faces dries our sweat, which will inevitably begin to pour at our next stop.

As usual, Samson is pressing hard on the gas pedal doing everything in his power to make up for lost time. It seems like we're perpetually late – whether it's trying to finish up a pastors meeting, squeezing in one more conversation with a widow who stopped by for food, or helping to arrange a marriage for one of my foster children (all in an average morning) – there's always something else to be done.

Hugging the edge of the tree-lined road, our caravan comes screeching to a halt - narrowly avoiding a collision with a herd of goats that were equally surprised. While most believe that goats make a "meh-meh" sound, I can tell you that a goat screams for its life when faced with the logo of a Tata minivan within inches of its face.

You never know what you'll encounter along the way.

Their owner, wearing nothing more than dusty sandals and a fabric lungi wrapped around his waist and pulled high up on his thighs, scurries back and forth tapping wayward goats with his long herding stick.

What feels like an Indian cultural safari for Westerners who come to visit is nothing more than "ordinary" in my team's daily life.

With the herd in our rear-view mirror, we notice a commotion stirring in the field off to our left. Jumping from tree to tree in the same direction we are traveling, a monkey has his eyes set on the near-ripe bananas hanging in giant clusters. Landing high in the treetop, he starts ripping fruit off by the fistful only to be startled by a yelling man swinging a bamboo pole in his direction.

"Leave! Leave!" the guard shouts over and over in Telagu, angrily chasing the monkey off.

He'll be back...the monkey and the man. Monkeys always come back, and the man inevitably comes chasing after him. They see an opportunity to grab food, and they'll do whatever it takes to get it. That same monkey (and some of his friends) will hide out in nearby trees waiting for the worker to dose off. When the coast is clear, the monkey sneaks back in to harvest a few more of his favorite treats. The truth is that the monkey is *compelled.*

He can't help it. He allows himself to be ruled by his natural urges to get whatever he wants – without regard to the needs or desires of the field owner. While I'm sure that humans have not evolved from monkeys, I am quite certain we are both compelled to get what we want in this life.

To be compelled means that we are "persuasively driven to be or do something."

The big difference between that monkey and us is that we have a choice as to what we will allow ourselves to be compelled by. The monkey is driven to do whatever it takes to get the bananas, but as human beings, we can make daily decisions about who we will be and what we will do with our lives.

We have the power to choose what we will be compelled by.

Coming to America

When I came to the United States for the first time in 1994, I was shocked! I couldn't believe what my eyes were seeing.

The pastor who was hosting me picked me up from the airport, and we immediately pulled on to what I would learn was a freeway. There were literally thousands of cars zooming back and forth heading in every direction. Where were all these people going in such a hurry?

I soon discovered they were commuting to faraway jobs, cruising to shopping malls, or simply driving around to get their baby to fall asleep. I had never even heard of such a thing.

Before heading to his home, he asked me if I wanted to stop for some food. Since I was famished after the 22-hour flight from Chennai, I agreed and began envisioning my wife's famous vegetable curry with a pile of steaming hot rice. Instead, we found ourselves pulling up to a McDonalds – something I had seen in the big city of Chennai, but never felt the urge to try.

"Welcome to McDonalds. May I help you?" squawked a mysterious voice from a round speaker mounted on a pole.

"What do you want?" asked my host as he turned and saw my eyes widened and my mind trying to assimilate exactly what was going on. "You can get a cheeseburger or a salad or some chicken nuggets. What sounds good?"

I kept scanning the lit-up board for vegetable curry, but it was nowhere to be found.

"I'll...I'll just have whatever you're having," I replied hesitantly.

"Okay, we'll take two number threes with large Diet Cokes," shouted the pastor.

I kept thinking to myself, "Why is he yelling at this box, and where is our food going to come from? Was it appearing out of that box somehow? And, what exactly is a number three?"

"That'll be $12.45. Go ahead and pull around to the first window," the box yelled back at us.

The pastor drove around, and I slowly started to put all the pieces together. I still couldn't believe that woman was handing our food out a window and into our car.

"Don't people go inside the restaurant to eat? Are they really in that big of a hurry they can't just sit down for a few minutes?" I asked.

I was quite sure I had landed in a totally different world – like another planet. While he was looking at me as if I was an alien, I kept thinking the exact same thing about him – and everyone else in that drive-thru.

Before coming to the US, I envisioned America as God's country, because it's a Christian nation. In my mind at the time, the only conceivable reason why everyone was so blessed was because everyone was a Christian.

The next day I realized how naïve my assumptions were about the "blessings" of the American people. It wasn't a sermon or a devotional or a Bible passage that opened my eyes.

It was a grocery store.

As we approached the front doors, they opened automatically as if to usher us in to Glory. There was even some guy named Gabriel handing us an ad on the way in. My hosts rushed past him and grabbed a cart to start filling it with items on his list. I stood in complete awe. My eyes were filled with row upon row of bottles, cans, and packages – all colorfully covered with brands I had never heard of.

There was
canned meat,
pre-packaged lettuce,
100 different types of soap,
and even something called Cheez Whiz.

More like "gee-whiz!" Just when I thought I was getting the hang of this whole drive-thru lifestyle of America, my mind was absolutely blown by the sights and sounds of something as simple as a grocery store. The place was as big as the ocean I had just crossed, and it was beyond my human comprehension to even know where to start.

Where we live in Tenali, my wife goes shopping in town. Walking from vendor to vendor (similar to a Western farmer's market), she selects the vegetables and spices we need for the day. Without refrigeration, we only buy what we'll immediately use. When we need rice, we go to the store that sells rice. If we want milk, we call a man to bring by a buffalo to milk the animal right on the spot to ensure its freshness. If we want fish, we go over by the river and purchase something that was freshly caught. If we want meat, we kill one of the chickens running around our own yard.

Can you imagine my heart pounding with anxiety as I walked up and down every aisle trying to fathom why someone would need so many choices?

Then, I realized.

It must be incredibly difficult to trust Jesus to provide for you and your family when you already have everything you need. When you have so many choices – whether on a drive-thru menu or in unending aisles of a grocery store – it can be easy to assume that the world simply revolves around what you want.

As I stood in the middle of that grocery store surrounded by things that I'll likely never eat, I had compassion for the people of the United States. Because of all these choices (and accompanying materialism), how easy it must be to think that life is all about "me."

While the materialism may be more prominent in the Western world, self-centeredness is no respecter of nations or persons. It can be seen just as well in my country or any other around the globe. You might just need to dig beneath the surface of culture to find it.

When we think that life is all about me and what I want, all of a sudden a monkey climbs up on our shoulders and becomes difficult to shake. It's the monkey that's compelled by his urge to get whatever he wants – without regard to the needs or desires of others. That metaphorical monkey on our backs can compel us to make decisions resulting in days, weeks, months, or even years of regret.

What may be just a cultural norm might stand in stark contrast to being the type of person you truly want to be – and ultimately who God created you to be. Without taking time to unearth what compels you and me, we're destined to allow that monkey to convince us we should just live for ourselves.

Four Things We're Tempted to Be Compelled By

When my friends from the West come to visit us in India, they are fascinated by the sight of a monkey – whether high up in a tree, along the road, or even on the back of a young owner. What they fail to realize is that the seemingly cute and playful animal can turn violent at any moment.

On one occasion, a team was visiting our ministry, and we were feeding a group of children living on the streets. As Lakshmi approached with a monkey on a leash, one of the Americans reached out take hold of the rope. Immediately, the monkey leaped off the ground onto his leg and started biting into his jeans. Yes, thankfully, he was wearing jeans, and he danced like Bollywood star – finally shaking that monkey loose.

While the children were laughing, the Americans were horrified at the possibility of contracting a disease that might never be shaken.

Monkeys are incredibly territorial when it comes to their owners. They will protect him or her by any means, because the monkey knows that their owner is the one who feeds them and cares for them. While some may assume that the human being owns the monkey, it is often vice versa.
You see where this is going, right?

WHAT IS COMPELLING YOU?

The Apostle Paul writes, *"Don't you know that when you offer yourselves to someone as obedient slaves, you are slaves of the one you obey - whether you are slaves to sin, which leads to death, or to obedience, which leads to righteousness?" (Romans 6:16 – NIV)*

When we allow ourselves to become enslaved to the monkey – to the desire to simply live for ourselves, we will be tempted to be someone who doesn't necessarily align with our identity as a follower of Jesus – one who has been deemed righteous in the sight of God.

There are four major temptations seeking to jump on our backs:

- **We're tempted to be SOOTHED.**

  So much of the focus on materialism and entertainment in our world is driven by a desire to be comforted. My guess is that you experience unending challenges of everyday life – getting the kids off to school, overcoming issues at work, fighting traffic, prepping dinner, wrestling through homework, and finally collapsing into bed – only to get up and do it all over again the next day.

  Who doesn't want to be soothed from all of that?

  The challenge comes when we're *compelled* to be soothed in ways that merely center on ourselves, and we continue to turn to the same things on an ongoing basis.

  Yes, that new gadget or outfit will make you feel better for a moment, but when your credit card bill starts to grow month after month, you know you've got a monkey on your back. Yes, that gallon of ice cream you dig in to right before bed will take off the edge, but when your doctor has concerns about your health, you know you've got a monkey on your back. And, yes, watching a marathon session of your favorite show on Netflix while simultaneously surfing Pinterest on your iPad is mind-numbing, but when your kids start to pull away from lack of attention, you know you've got a monkey on your back.

  The truth is God has given us the ability and desire to take pleasure in life, and all of these things are to be enjoyed – whether it's physical possessions, food, or entertainment.

The challenge comes when we're compelled to be soothed by these things time and again. Turning to our comforts over and over is a signal that we're seeking Peace from a source that can't truly provide it.

- **We're tempted to be POWERFUL.**

  "Me? Power-hungry? I'm not interested in being President or running a multi-national company any time soon." That type of aggressive drivenness may not be compelling you, but power comes in many forms.

  Do you have a need to always be right?
  Do you look down on others who don't hold your same views?
  Do you withhold forgiveness when you've been wronged?
  Do you take advantage of people who are willing to work for little money?

  These are all subtle (and not so subtle) ways we feel better than others around us. This pseudo-power pumps up our self-esteem for a moment – yet withers as soon as we realize someone else is better, stronger, faster, richer, prettier, or smarter than us in whatever category we're seeking to compare ourselves.

  This monkey is only be shaken when we come to an understanding that our identity can be found as humanity's servant - ultimately a role that's even more powerful.

- **We're tempted to be LIKED.**

  From the time we enter grade school, we want to fit in with a certain group of people. You may not have wanted the admiration of the popular kids, but we all seem to have a desire to be liked at some level.

  In your effort to fit in, to what lengths have you been willing to go? Spent crazy amounts of money on a certain brand of jeans? Listened to a band just because everyone else was into it? Joined in on conversations about someone even though you felt uncomfortable about it? Made borderline unethical decisions at work just to fit in with your team? Ignored your values to simply go along with everyone else? It's so easy to do.

  Unfortunately, this monkey can grip us so tight we lose sight of who we are and what we really stand for. We should be admired – not because we necessarily fit in with what everyone else is doing – but because of our character and the choices we make, which are motivated by our love for others.

- **We're tempted to be LOVED.**

  When I first came to America, one of the things that shocked me even more than drive-thru restaurants and the endless selection at the grocery store was the degree to which sexuality is flaunted openly.

  Rather than something sacred to be celebrated between a husband and wife, it is being cheapened into nothing more than tool of advertising or something to be conquered with a one-night stand. When we're lured in by sexy advertising or choose to participate in selfish expressions of sexual pleasure, we're pursuing love and connection in a way that will never ultimately satisfy.

There's nothing unusual about being compelled by all of these things at some level. Yet, just because it's normal doesn't mean that it aligns with who you are as a child of God. Maybe we could choose something even better.

What Can We Be Compelled By?

When you get up in the morning, what motivates you to get going? What drives you to do whatever it is you do?

If you've read through the book of Acts, you'll discover a man named Paul who was compelled in everything he did. He was motivated to be a well-studied Jew with a dedication to his religion. With the arrival of a new sect (followers of Jesus), he was driven to track them down to have them punished and even killed. Yet, when he encountered the power and love of Jesus on the road to Damascus, what compelled Paul radically changed.

In that divine encounter, the monkey was shaken off his back, and God miraculously re-directed his steps. Instead of being driven to follow his own selfish desires, he was driven toward a life of service for the benefit of others.

He writes, *"For Christ's love compels us, because we are convinced that one died for all, and therefore all died. And he died for all, that those who live should no longer live for themselves but for him who died for them and was raised again." (2 Corinthians 5:14-15 – NIV)*

Jesus' love compelled Paul. Why? Because Jesus died on Paul's behalf. It was Jesus' ultimate act of sacrificial love that drove Paul to no longer live for himself, but to live for Christ. To live for Christ means to focus on what He found to be the most important thing in this life.

When asked what the greatest commandment was, Jesus replied, *"Love the Lord your God with all your heart and with all your soul and with all your mind. This is the first and greatest commandment. And the second is like it: 'Love your neighbor as yourself." (Matthew 22:37-38 – NIV)*

This is what it means to have Christ's love compel us. Christ loved us when we were at our worst, and we now have the opportunity to be a conduit of His love to everyone around us. This is what I'm staking my life on.

It would be so easy to allow a monkey to climb up on my back and compel me to live just for myself, but it's because of Christ's love that I'm compelled to live for Him and for my neighbors, the closest of which happen to live in thousands of villages in southern India.

Posing with gypsy women during rural village ministry.

Did you know that over 70% of India's population lives in 550,000 villages? As the second-most populated country in the world with over 1.3 billion people, our nation speaks 19 different languages and almost 900 local dialects. 80% of the population is Hindu, while 13% are Muslim, and a mere 3% are Christian.

As you can see, I have my work cut out for me.

After traveling to the US and UK for the first time, people started joining us in India for short trips to witness the powerful things that God is doing through our ministries. When I sit down with them in their home country, I try to share how expansive our work is, but it's not until they actually show up on the scene that they're able to take in the true breadth.

Inevitably, each person always asks, "How do you do it? How are you able to do all this stuff?"

My answer is always the same, "It's because of God's grace."

Although that statement is 100% true, it's a bit of an easy way out of explaining that we have chosen to live a different type of life. If I took the time to look each person in the eye and say "we have chosen to avoid living a materialistic, self-centered life focused on comfort and entertainment", it probably wouldn't go over too well.

I would rather have them witness a radically different kind of lifestyle and be impacted at such a deep level that they'll never forget their experience in India. Although I want each person to walk away with a 'road to Damascus' kind of experience, I also know that explaining what we do in words can be helpful as well.

This book is my effort to share why we do what we do at Harvest India and how we have chosen to live our lives. It's an invitation to join us on the adventure of being compelled by the love of Christ. It's a challenge to examine what you're being compelled by right now.

In the upcoming chapters, I will share what compels my leadership and me, but there are many other God-honoring motivations that can drive us as followers of Jesus. As you are courageous to examine what compels you, I want to offer up several questions that may be helpful in the process.

1. Does it honor God?

God created us, loves us, and has our best interest in mind. At the core of His message to Moses was that the people should put no other gods before Him. In other words, God was to be honored as the one true God – the only One to be exalted, praised, worshipped, and revered. Nothing has changed for us as followers of Jesus. So, the question is, whatever is compelling you, does it honor God as the One to be held high above all else?

2. Does it serve the best interests of others?

At the heart of what compelled Paul was a choice not to live for himself any longer. He chose to live for Christ, which meant he would join Jesus in a ministry of serving others. With a natural inclination to be self-centered, we have that message reinforced by our culture encouraging us to buy what we want, pursue what's best for us, and live however we choose. What about those around you? How are the things that compel you ultimately impacting your spouse, children, family, friends, and your neighbors (near and far)?

3. Does it respect and care for your body, mind, and soul?

You and I only get one body in this life. Although medical professionals have made incredible strides toward the replacement of almost any body part, there's nothing like taking care of ourselves over the long haul.

Paul writes, *"Do you not know that your bodies are temples of the Holy Spirit, who is in you, whom you have received from God? You are not your own; you were bought at a price. Therefore honor God with your bodies." (1 Corinthians 6:19-20 – NIV)*

Ironically, this passage is in the context of sexual immorality, but it holds true when we think about how we treat every part of our being. From our physical body to our mind and soul, every part of us is sacred. Does the thing that's compelling you care for your body, mind, and soul – or tear it down?

4. Does it produce lasting joy and peace within you?

Many things can give us a hit of momentary happiness or pleasure, but don't you want to be compelled by things that provide lasting results?

When you think about what is motivating you in life, are the outcomes fleeting or long-lasting? Is it something you turn to over and over again to reproduce a feeling that goes away quickly? Rich, healthy experiences seem to build on one another rather than evaporating time after time. Aim for that which lasts.

5. Does it flow from your identity as a child of God?

As a follower of Jesus, you have been adopted into the family of God, and you have been given a new identity. Not only have you been created by God, but you are considered a child of God. Therefore, you have access to all the resources your Father in heaven has to offer and can live in light of that reality. You are fully forgiven, loved, blessed, and destined to greatness. Whatever compels you should flow from your new identity.

6. Does it align with the principles of the Scriptures?

As a follower of Jesus, this is a critical question to ask ourselves. While Jesus is the One we follow, we believe that the Bible is a collection of ancient writings inspired by God to give us direction in our daily lives. We want to be compelled by things that align with the values and principles we see exhibited in the life and ministry of Jesus and the apostles. If we're being driven by something that is out of alignment with the Bible, it is cause to question whether that monkey needs to be shaken loose from our back.

My guess is you're feeling a bit challenged right now, and you should. I am as well. This book is designed to be a manifesto – a message to the nations – calling all of us to something more as followers of Jesus. My deepest desire is that this would be more than a collection of 10 things that inspire and motivate me. I invite you to be compelled by these statements as well.

I actually believe this stuff, and I choose to live it out on a daily basis. If I'm just reading about it in the Bible and not compelled by it, what's the point? If I'm simply teaching it on Sundays and not experiencing it firsthand, I'm just sharing information with people around me. There is a big difference between calling oneself a Christian and actually choosing to follow Jesus and allow His love to compel us. That's what my life and ministry are all about.

I'm far from perfect, but I know what I'm compelled by.
Do you?

SMALL GROUP WEEK #1

Getting Started

1. Share a "high" and a "low" from your week – something that went good and something that went not-so-good. (Go around the room allowing each person to have time to check-in and share.)

2. Have you ever been to India before? If so, what did you experience? If not, what do you know about the country?

3. Suresh shared about several experiences that shocked or confused him about the West. What are some other things that would surprise someone from outside your culture?

Going Deeper

4. Read Romans 6:1-14. What stands out to you in this passage?

5. What does it mean to be a "slave to sin"?

6. If our "old self was crucified with him", then why do so many of us struggle with being slaves to sin?

7. Suresh described four common temptations that become like a monkey on our backs – enslaving us to live for ourselves. We're tempted to be soothed, powerful, liked, and loved. If you need to, go back and read over the descriptions. Which one are you most tempted to be enslaved by?

8. Instead of being enslaved by these temptations, Suresh suggested that we can live a compelling life. Read 2 Corinthians 5:14-15. What does it practically look like to live a life compelled by Christ's love?

Applying It To Your Life

9. To discover what currently compels you, think about the people, places, and things in your life. You have chosen each one of them for a reason. Even if it's by 'default', you've allowed them (spouse, friends, job, home, car, clothes, hobbies, etc.) to be there for a reason. As you think about these things, what do you sense is compelling you the most in your life?

10. As you think about what's compelling you, take a moment to re-read the six questions at the end of the chapter. Which question do you find most challenging, and why?

11. What's the one thing that you want to take away from our group time today?

CHAPTER 2

I AM COMPELLED TO FOLLOW JESUS WHEREVER HE LEADS

None of us choose the family we are born into, but there's no doubt that those early years shape us tremendously. God chose for me to be born in the city of Tenali in southern India. My father was a Hindu belonging to a high-caste, and my mother, Lalitha Kumari, came from a Christian family – considered to be the lowest of all castes.

Despite their best efforts, my parent's marriage ended in divorce – largely due to the pressure mounting from both of their families. My father's mother was adamant that he should have married a Hindu girl of the same caste, and he eventually left my Mom to do so when I was just six years old.

I have no memory of him – nor any information about his life.

In India, divorce is quite rare, and when my parents separated, it was almost unheard of. Despite the stigma of her situation, my Mom completed three years of nursing school and landed a well-respected job for a Christian woman – working in a local hospital. I still remember her wearing a bright-white sari as she headed off to work each day.

Like many young people who grow up in a Christian home, faith is something passed along from one's parents, but not always fully embraced. There comes a time when each of us must decide whether we will choose to follow in the footsteps of the One who died on our behalf.

For my Mom, that moment came at a Gospel crusade as she listened to a traveling evangelist challenge the hundreds present…

> *Jesus is telling us, "Whoever wants to be my disciple must deny themselves and take up their cross daily and follow me. For whoever wants to save their life will lose it, but whoever loses their life for me will save it." (Luke 9:23-24 – NIV)*
>
> *My question for you tonight is…are you willing to follow Jesus wherever He leads? Are you willing to lose the life you have for the life He wants to give you? Are you willing to follow Him for the rest of your days?*
>
> *Stand up if you want to serve the Lord all your life.*

My Mom immediately stood up that night in response to God's call on her life. She believed with all her heart that if she left everything behind, God would take care of her needs in the present and reward her in the life to come.

Because my Mom knew without a doubt she was called to minister, she began planning to attend a Bible college several hours away from our home. With no adequate accommodations for children on the campus, she reached out to her five brothers and two sisters to ask if my brother, Sudheer, and I could live with one of them.

Every one of them turned their backs on her…and us.

They couldn't fathom why she would leave her career and even her children to pursue God's call on her life. Frankly, you might not understand it either.

At the ages of seven and ten, my brother and I were placed in an orphanage as our Mom headed off to prepare for ministry. Over the next year, my grandfather, Boaz, and grandmother, Rachel, would come to visit us several times a week, and we would usually spend the weekend with them at their home as well. Although they would have loved to take us in, his police pension of 70 rupees a month (the equivalent of a dollar) wasn't enough to supply everything we would have needed.

TO FOLLOW JESUS WHEREVER HE LEADS

While I have many positive memories of my 'brothers and sisters' at the children's home, I held a bitterness in my heart toward God about the divisions within our family. Not only had my father disappeared, but my mother left to attend school and none of our family was willing to take us in. With this pain in my heart, I compensated by being a good, Christian boy who focused on his studies and did everything that was expected of him.

I know what you're thinking.

"How could a loving mother ever leave behind her children in an orphanage? Why is he only upset at God and his family? Why isn't he angry with his mother?"

My Mom - Lalitha Kumari

COMPELLED

I've been asked this on a number of occasions, and here's what I know. My Mom was incredibly courageous to quit her job and pursue ministry. She was making choices in light of the fact that Jesus was calling her to prepare for a life of service to the poor. Although it may be difficult to understand for a Western mind, the temporary separation of a child from his or her parents isn't that unusual. Indian children are regularly sent to boarding school for a quality education, and while this wasn't exactly the case for my brother and me, it was within the realm of cultural possibilities.

After completing her education, my Mom moved back to Tenali and started to travel and preach the Gospel in rural villages, and she would come and see us once or twice a month at the children's home.

High School

When I graduated from high school, I had no intention or interest in working for God. Instead, pursuing a successful job and an easy life, I stayed locally to attend college and began working toward a BA in Sociology.

My Mom was quite disappointed in me for not having an interest in serving the Lord. To appease her wishes, I would join her every summer break to travel from village to village to host evangelistic meetings.

Because we spent very little time with one another after my brother and I moved into the children's home, these summer adventures were an intimate experience between my Mom and I. Of course, she was very passionate and persistent about what she believed, and we would get into it from time to time. If she believed something, she was willing to do anything to back it up – even to the point of death.

During those late nights tearing down after the crusades, I would think to myself, "How long can we go on living like this? We're like gypsy people traveling from village to village without a home of our own." My Mom was always encouraging us saying, "There will be a time when God will honor our labor. This is our time to work, and God will bless us."

Although I enjoyed being with my Mom, I was always thankful for my summer break to come to an end.

TO FOLLOW JESUS WHEREVER HE LEADS

Drowning in His Grace

During my weekend breaks from college, I would often find myself back at my grandparent's home – the only sense of 'home' I really had. On this particular Saturday, my cousin, Howard, stopped by to see me. (Yes, that's his real name.) He kept nagging me to go explore a canal down the road aways, but I resisted.

I had no interest in traipsing through a canal, nor did I have any business being near rushing water since I didn't know how to swim.

After finally giving in to his hounding, we took off on a ten-minute walk and came to the water's edge. As we teetered down the narrow path running alongside the swift-moving water, he and I kidded each other about who was going to get wet first.

In a split second, the ground beneath our sandals gave way, and the slippery slope delivered us deep into the canal. With neither of us knowing how to swim, we began to thrash around as the current pulled us downstream. Our heads were bobbing up and down as our arms flailed about – grasping the air – trying to pull ourselves upward.

During those five minutes - what seemed like an eternity, I kept gasping for just one more breath. Convinced I was going to die beneath the surface, I knew that Jesus was my only hope. As I called out to God – begging Him to save my life, I blacked out under the murky depths.

Choking up water as a stranger pushed on my chest, my eyes opened to a horrendous scene. I'm not sure who dragged me out of the water, but I'll never forget watching the fisherman pull my cousin out of the canal…dead.

As two men carried us both back to my grandfather's home, I couldn't help but wonder why God had chosen to spare my life - and not the life of my cousin.

With Howard's body stretched out on the ground in front of the home, I could hear the distant sound of a popular radio program with Dr. R.R.K. Murthy. As I stared at his lifeless frame, the words of a popular Telagu song filled my ears…

"Jesus left the Glory and came down as a man to this world, because he loves you and cares for you."

Tears began to flow down my cheeks as I cried out to God. "Why did you save me?" I kept saying over and over. In the days to come, God started to shine a light on my selfishness and the choice I had made to follow my own agenda – specifically not to serve Him. On the outside, I was a good person who appeared to be a Christian, but my heart wasn't in a good place. I was doing all the right things for all the wrong reasons. I was behaving to please my professors and my Mom, but I wasn't interested in what God wanted for my life.

When God has a plan for someone's life, He will get your attention – no matter what it takes.

At 21 years of age, I knew God set me aside to make it clear that I was to follow Jesus wherever He leads. I soon finished my BA in Sociology, and I moved to Bangalore (about 10 hours away) to attend a Bible college. It was there I met a wonderful Christian girl who captured my attention at first sight. Although arranged marriages are common even among Christians in India, there was something about Cristina that was irresistible.

Cristina and I on our wedding day

TO FOLLOW JESUS WHEREVER HE LEADS

After finishing my M.Div. and getting married, we moved back to Tenali to live at the home of my grandfather who had recently passed away. My Mom's dream of seeing her sons join her in the ministry had finally come to fruition. Not only had Christina and I chosen to work alongside her, but so had my brother, Sudheer, who had finished studying with Youth With a Mission.

Just like my mother, we trusted God to provide for everything we needed each step of the way – from food to clothing to medical care. Instead of getting a job and squeezing ministry in on the weekends, we devoted every waking minute to seeing the Good News of Jesus Christ introduced to village after village. We saw God truly provide for all our needs.

During my first year of ministry with my Mom, we started a Bible school, and seven students joined us for a one-year program. Not only did they come to study, but they lived with us and ministered together in villages.

Can you imagine getting married, graduating from Bible college, moving back to your home town, and starting a Bible school all in the same year? I did mention that we had seven strangers move in with us to prepare to be sent out as pastors, right?

Eventually, the number of students and visiting faculty (friends from my Bible college days) just got to be too much, and we needed a second home to house the ministry.

Through the faithful generosity of David Prosser from New Life Ministries in the United Kingdom, we were able to pay for the home and cover the needs of the students as well. As an evangelist, he would come to Tenali for an entire month every year, and he joined us for 10 years straight.

David was willing to follow Jesus wherever He led, and the results were tremendous.

Not only did God fill his heart with a clear vision to impact the nation of India, but David was willing to share that calling with other people so they would partner with him financially. On top of that, he was committed to traveling to a faraway place for an entire month each year – away from his family and friends – to share the love of Jesus with people he didn't even know.

Because a white man was coming from a distant country, thousands of Hindus were drawn to listen to David and ultimately received the love and forgiveness of Jesus Christ as we hosted gospel meetings over those years. Because of his investment in our first Bible school, many pastors were educated, and numerous churches were started in rural villages by those same men and women.

David Prosser with my mother and family

What a tremendous example of being compelled to follow Jesus wherever He leads!

Why I'm Willing to Follow Jesus Wherever He Leads

Do you remember playing that school yard game of "follow the leader" as a kid? Of course, it was exciting to be the leader and make people go up and down over blazing hot playground equipment or through the thorny bushes – all in the name of fun.

Being willing to follow someone else meant that you were choosing to submit to whatever path they led you down. The truth is there's no place I'd rather be than where Jesus leads, and here's why…

- **Jesus has a plan for my life.**

  When I'm not sure which direction my life is headed, I know that Jesus isn't going to lead me astray. Rather than choosing my own path, I have come to the conclusion that His plan is much better. He has the big picture in mind while I can only see my immediate challenges. By the very fact that He says, *"Follow me"* to each of his disciples (including you and me), I am confident that He knows where He's taking me.

- **Jesus has my best interest in mind.**

He is not asking us to follow Him in order to take advantage of us or kill us. Jesus says, *"I have come that they may have life, and have it to the full."* This is His plan for my life!

Because Christ saved me from the deep waters like Jonah, I have a faith that Jesus will care for me, and He can handle anything I encounter in life. Even though many people in my life abandoned me at an early age, Jesus has never left my side. He has my back, and I have a confidence that He'll take care of me no matter what.

- **Jesus gives me confidence and hope.**

If Jesus has a plan for my life and my best interest in mind, then I can be confident that things are going to come together, and I can be filled with hope when everything around me may seem bleak.
Paul writes, *"Now faith is confidence in what we hope for and assurance about what we do not see." (Hebrews 11:1 – NIV)*

I may not see the solution to my problems with human eyes quite yet, but I have faith that Jesus has everything under control. There's no need to worry when I have a confidence that Jesus has everything I need.

- **Jesus is always on time.**

Although I might start to sweat when I don't see things coming together in my timing, I know that Jesus is never late. He is an on-time God! We are reminded, *"Let us not become weary in doing good, for at the proper time we will reap a harvest if we do not give up." (Galatians 6:9 – NIV)*
If something hasn't come to fruition quite yet in our lives, it's probably not God's timing.

When I add all this up, it tells me that I can trust Him. It tells me that there is no other place I'd rather be than where Jesus leads. Can you say that out loud with me?

COMPELLED

There's no place I'd rather be
than where Jesus leads.

Maybe you need to write that sentence down and post it on your mirror or dashboard. I find that saying these words out loud guides the trajectory of my heart. When I say them, I think to myself, "Yeah, that's right. There is no better place." It cultivates the natural question of, "Where is Jesus leading me?" It nudges me to tune my heart into the leading of the Holy Spirit and requires me to slow down and not just assume that I know where I'm going.

I can be confident in Jesus' plan, path, and power, but He calls for both my trust and my obedience.

When I was a little boy, I remember a time when we didn't have any food in our home or any money to go buy some. I'm not talking about opening up your fridge or pantry and not seeing anything that looks appetizing. We didn't even have a refrigerator! Until the age of 10, I grew up in a mud floor, thatched-roof home that only had a single room. And, in this case, there wasn't a single thing to eat in our house – no rice and no curry.

"Mom, what are we going to eat?" I asked.

"Our food will be ready soon," she replied with confidence in her voice.

I was hungry and confused, because I didn't see any food in our house nor anything cooking in the pot. As we lay on our cots under the fan, I noticed my Mom crying out to God – asking Him to provide for our needs. Within the hour, our neighbor, Jeevamma, knocked on the open door and walked on in. "What are you and the boys having for lunch?" she asked my mother.

When she realized we didn't have anything to eat, Jeevamma brought over a huge, delicious meal, and we had more than enough to eat. It's been over 40 years since then, and I remember it like it was yesterday.

This is what our God does. He never leaves us or forsakes us. He sees what we need, and He is our provision. I saw my Mom model this type of deep confidence in God throughout her life, and I learned how to trust Him from her example. I've witnessed Him deliver me and others time after time, and I'm confident that He'll keep doing it as we follow wherever He leads.

TO FOLLOW JESUS WHEREVER HE LEADS

How to Follow Jesus Wherever He Leads
It's wonderful to read about Jesus and express our love to Him at church, but until we're willing to follow him wherever He leads, we're missing out on our role as His representatives in this world.

In The Message, it reads, *"God put the world square with himself through the Messiah, giving the world a fresh start by offering forgiveness of sins. God has given us the task of telling everyone what he is doing. We're Christ's representatives. God uses us to persuade men and women to drop their differences and enter into God's work of making things right between them. We're speaking for Christ himself now: Become friends with God; he's already a friend with you." (2 Corinthians 5:19-20 – MSG)*

Are you kidding me? We get to be representatives of Jesus and speak love on His behalf? That's exactly right! The Apostle Paul is saying, "You're already friends with God, and now you get to go around helping other people be friends with God, too."

God may not be calling you to leave your job like my Mom, and you may not have an underwater meeting with Jesus like me, but God is calling you to be His ambassador in this world. He needs men and women to listen to His voice saying "Follow me" and be willing to say, "Here I am, Lord. Send me!"

Following Jesus wherever He leads doesn't happen by accident. It requires me to be in tune with what He desires and my obedience when I hear His voice. Over the years, I've developed a rhythm that positions me to listen and follow.

1. **We start our day with prayer and study.**

   I know this may sound crazy, but my wife and I get up at 4:30am every day to pray and study the Scriptures. From our little home on the main campus of our ministry, we walk about 100 yards up to the church and climb the stairs to stand on the top and look out over the land God has given us.

   We begin by expressing our love for God out loud and calling out the great qualities that He possesses. We're not telling God anything He doesn't already know, but we're calling to mind the truth for ourselves. As we worship Him and confess our sins, we're reminding our hearts to recognize He is God and we are not. His plan is the one to follow – not our own. It is a process of submission to His will.

Then, we pray for the 1,300+ children in our care and the 1,500+ pastors and churches within our ministry. We pray for our city, our nation, and our world. And, yes, we even pray for you!

At 5:30am, we go back to our home and wake up the kids. We sing songs together as they wipe sleep from their eyes, and we read the Scriptures together. Oftentimes, the children will sing a song by themselves and recite the Bible verses they're memorizing for the week.

You may find this to be far beyond what you could imagine for your family, but may I remind you that we all have the power to set the 'norm' in our households.

2. We listen to what Jesus is calling us to do.

Not only are we listening to God through the Scriptures, but we're paying close attention to what we sense Jesus wants for us and from us. His "still, small voice" can come through impressions during times of prayer, the illumination of our Bible reading, conversations with friends or family, and even supernatural insights from other followers of Jesus.

There are many ways that Jesus can speak to us, but the question is, "Are we listening?" Do we have our antennas up – ready to hear from Him?

It goes without saying that anything we sense Jesus calling us to do should align with the principles that we read in the Bible. Unfortunately, some people don't think that Jesus still speaks to us, so they've stopped listening altogether.

What if you just asked a simple question, "Jesus, where do you want to lead me today?" I dare you. Ask, and see what happens.

3. We seek to respond with obedience and confidence.

Sometimes, things are quite clear. We have a basic understanding that Jesus wants us to be honest, trustworthy, and forgiving. Yes, we want to be those things.

But, what about how we use our time? How is Jesus calling us to spend our money? Who does He want me to love in a practical way? These are the questions that don't necessarily have clear answers straight from the Bible, but we believe Jesus can (and does) guide us based on what He's uniquely doing in each of our lives. When we sense His leading, we seek to respond with obedience as quickly and as best we can.

I know that word "obedience" is far from in vogue in the West (or probably anywhere else), but it's at the heart of what it means to be a follower of Jesus.

John writes, *"And this is love: that we walk in obedience to his commands. As you have heard from the beginning, his command is that you walk in love." (2 John 1:6 – NIV)*

As we obediently follow the leading of Jesus, we have great confidence that He is experienced and dependable guide. His main plan for our lives is to give us life to the full. Why wouldn't we want to trust Him?

As a side note, this whole "listen and obey" thing can be a little tricky. We sometimes head down a road that doesn't exactly turn out the way we envisioned. Was it the 'wrong' decision? Maybe – maybe not. Your desire was to follow Jesus' leading, right? Then, I believe that He sees your heart, and you're learning in the process – just like I am. Give yourself grace, and keep listening and obeying.

The Example of the Rich Man

Let's look at an example from the Bible of someone who had the chance to listen and obey. In Matthew 19:16-22, Jesus is approached by a wealthy man who asks Him a question:

Just then a man came up to Jesus and asked, "Teacher, what good thing must I do to get eternal life?"

"Why do you ask me about what is good?" Jesus replied. "There is only One who is good. If you want to enter life, keep the commandments."

I think Jesus knew where this conversation was going. The rich man wanted to make sure he was destined for heaven, but Jesus knew what was going on in the man's heart.

"Which ones?" he inquired.

Jesus replied, "'You shall not murder, you shall not commit adultery, you shall not steal, you shall not give false testimony, honor your father and mother,' and 'love your neighbor as yourself.'"

"All these I have kept," the young man said. "What do I still lack?"

Come on! Who has actually kept all those commandments their entire life?

Jesus answered, "If you want to be perfect, go, sell your possessions and give to the poor, and you will have treasure in heaven. Then come, follow me." When the young man heard this, he went away sad, because he had great wealth.

Notice the two key words: "Follow me." Jesus knew what was gripping the man's heart, and He invited him to let go of it. This man was practicing religion – going to church and being a good person, but Jesus was calling for an act of surrender. Jesus was calling him to shift where he was placing his trust, but the man couldn't shake that monkey off his back. He probably continued to be a 'good person' in the eyes of others, but he was missing out on the adventure of following on the heels of Jesus.

Jesus says, *"Take my yoke upon you and learn from me, for I am gentle and humble in heart, and you will find rest for your souls. For my yoke is easy and my burden is light." (Matthew 11:29-30 – NIV)*

By relinquishing his wealth, he would have surrendered his life and received the gift of a lightened load. Instead, he perceived Jesus' offer as a requirement that was too heavy to bear. How often is that the case with us?

We sense Jesus is calling us to do something, but we feel overwhelmed or anxious about it. In reality, Jesus isn't trying to burden us, but guide us with an easy yoke. The reason why following Christ always costs something is because He wants us to give up that which weighs us down and holds us back. As a follower of Jesus, obedience to His calling is assumed.

Otherwise, we are simply following ourselves and whatever it is we're seeking to hold on to - riches in the case of the man in this passage. Whatever we're gripping will never give us true and lasting life. It will rob us of God's best plan. The enemy's scheme is to convince us that Jesus' path is ludicrous and not something any right-minded person would ever pursue. You may hear the enemy saying, "It's just too fanatical."

I can imagine that the rich man was thinking that to himself. "I can't give up everything I've worked for. That's just too much to ask."

He was blind to the fact that there was something so much better to put his trust in. Freedom comes from following Jesus and having a confidence in His plan for your life. Remember, Jesus didn't call us to be comfortable in this world. He calls us to be obedient.

Your greatest fear may be that God will call you to go to Africa, India, the job you may not love, or in my case – the US or UK. I'm reminded of this every time I get on a plane to travel around the other side of the globe. While I love giving an update to our supporters because it helps them see how God is at work through their donations, I would much rather stay in my comfort zone in India – eating my wife's curry - and focusing on our day-to-day ministry.

When I cried out to God underneath the water, I never dreamed He would send me to places where I would be forced to eat Chicken McNuggets, walk through malls where I couldn't afford to buy anything, or freeze to death in 65 degree weather. I would much rather be sitting outside my two-room home surrounded by 1,300 children in 100 degree heat.

Isn't it funny how God calls us out of what's familiar to use us in extraordinary ways?

When Jesus obeyed God the Father, He left the heavens, and He experienced turmoil, pain, and even rejection – motivated by a deep love for you and for me. In the midst of His challenges, Jesus trusted the Father to provide everything He needed. He trusted the Father's plan and purpose. Following Jesus is about trusting Him with your life, your path, and your future. What are you trusting in other than Jesus? Are you trusting in your education, your title, your home, your possessions, or even your family?

No matter where I travel, I see people (even Christians) pursuing a 'feel-good' life – putting their trust in so many things other than Jesus. We may not indulge in a hedonistic lifestyle, but instead we turn to religious experiences to satisfy that spiritual hunger within all of us. By attending church a couple of times a month and even tossing a few bucks in the offering, we give ourselves a temporary spiritual fix while remaining deaf to Jesus' still, small voice of guidance.

Instead of listening closely and following hard after Jesus, many of us are looking for temporary solutions and shortcuts - far from actually following the life and teachings of our Savior.

I can tell you want more than that. You love Jesus, and you want to hear His voice. When you hear his voice, you are compelled to respond with, "Yes, Lord. Send me!"

My guess is that Jesus has been nudging you to do something outside your comfort zone, and you've been taking your time to respond. It's probably the first thing that came to mind as you read this chapter. Maybe it's starting to take your relationship with Him seriously. Or, perhaps, it's forgiving someone who has wounded you deeply. Possibly, he's calling you to join or start a ministry to a group who is in need.

I don't know what it is, but you're probably a bit anxious if you've been stalling.

Remember, Jesus has your best interest in mind, and He'll provide all the resources you'll need along the way – including wisdom, strength, and power. You are His child, and He wants you to experience a full and abundant life. Jesus has called you to be His representative – going here and there upon the Earth – dispensing His love to people in a need.

He is worthy of our trust. Let's follow Jesus together - wherever He leads. Will you join me?

SMALL GROUP WEEK #2

Getting Started

1. As you think about this season of your life, what are you most thankful for, and why?

2. When you read about Suresh's mother and her decision to go to Bible school without her two boys, what was your initial reaction?

3. When Suresh almost drowned in the river and his cousin didn't survive, God used the tragic event to get his attention. Have you ever experienced something challenging that opened your eyes to life or faith in a new way? What was it like?

Going Deeper

4. Read Matthew 4:18-22 and then reflect on this quote for a moment, "There's no place I'd rather be than where Jesus leads." Do you think James and John believed this statement before or after following Jesus? Do you believe that statement yourself?

5. Suresh gives several reasons why Jesus is worthy of our trust:

   a. Jesus has a plan for my life.
   b. Jesus has my best interest in mind.
   c. Jesus gives me confidence and hope.
   d. Jesus is always on time.

   Which one of these statements is easiest for you to embrace? Which one is the hardest to believe?

6. Read Matthew 19:16-23. What would you say was compelling this man's life?

7. If we were able to interview this man after his encounter with Jesus, what do you think he would say?

Applying It To Your Life

8. The rich man was being weighed down by his wealth, and Jesus was trying to lighten his load so the man could follow Him. What do you sense is weighing you down from following Jesus wherever He leads?

9. What have you been resisting recently that God has been nudging you to do?

10. What would it practically look like to start trusting Jesus to lead you in that direction this week?

CHAPTER 3

I AM COMPELLED BY GOD'S VISION FOR MY LIFE

As I climb out of the van in a rush to meet with a village elder who is waiting for me, my eyes are drawn to a frail woman slowly making her way down the windy path to the right of our vehicle. With a walking stick in her left hand and a bucket in the right, she takes one careful step after another – making sure the precious water she had just hoisted out of the well doesn't spill as she heads back home.

A normal scene in India. Yet, something isn't quite right with this woman. It isn't her hunched posture, her gnarled hands, or even her turtle-like pace that captures my attention.

It is her vision.

As my team and I begin to hurry by her, I notice cloudiness in both eyes that must be like trying to see through a fogged-up window on a rainy day. I immediately turn around and stop the woman.

"Ma'am, can you see me?" I ask her in Telagu.

With a feeble voice matching the frailty of her frame, she turns and says, "Young man, I haven't been able to see anything clearly for years."

That's the case for many of the elderly men and women in our country who slowly lose their vision due to cataracts – a haze or fogginess that develops in the eye lens. A normally clear lens allows light to pass through to the back of the eye so that we can see well-defined images. In this case, both of her eyes are almost completely opaque, and she can only see well enough to avoid large objects heading in her direction. In developing countries such as India, a high incidence of eye disease is caused by malnutrition, inadequate health services, poor drinking water, and a lack of sanitation.

"Do you want to see clearly again?" I ask.

"That is not possible, my son," she whispers as she keeps walking.

Solomon, the wisest man who ever lived, tells us, *"Where there is no vision, the people perish…" (Proverbs 29:18 – KJV)*

This is not only true in the case of physical eyesight with so many of the elderly I dearly love, but it's true when it comes to our entire lives.

We need to have a clear vision of what God is doing in our lives so that we can collaborate with Him. Notice the word "collaboration" literally means to co-labor. By trusting God with His vision, we have the opportunity to join Him in the work He is doing in us and through us.

I believe God has both a general and specific vision for each one of us.

God's General Vision For You and Me

As we read the Scriptures, it becomes incredibly clear what God's "general" vision (or purpose) for our lives is through the Great Commandment and the Great Commission.

- **Love God = Obey God.**

  Specifically, Jesus calls us to *"Love the Lord your God with all your heart and with all your soul and with all your mind." (Matthew 22:37 – NIV)* He tells us this is the first and greatest commandment. To love God in this holistic way means that we're submitting every aspect of our lives to Him – not just a mushy-gushy teenage crush evidenced by goose bumps during worship and underlining in your Bible.

Jesus is talking about a love for God that results in obedience.

"Anyone who loves me will obey my teaching. My Father will love them, and we will come to them and make our home with them. Anyone who does not love me will not obey my teaching. These words you hear are not my own; they belong to the Father who sent me." (John 14:23-24 – NIV)

The idea that obedience and love are connected may seem foreign to you. Obedience can seem like such a harsh word, can't it? Something associated with force, coercion, and possible punishment. While God's love for us is unconditional, Jesus makes it clear that obedience is the evidence we have more than a youthful affection toward our Creator.

In India, it is well known that Western culture places a heavy emphasis on the emotions of love (and often promiscuity) – generally more so than the quality of commitment. It's one of the reasons Indian conservatives have resisted the infiltration of the Hallmark-inspired Valentine's Day into our country. Our God-given emotions are beautiful and healthy, but a mature love is rooted in dedication and personal action for the benefit of another.

When we choose to submit our lives to the leadership of Jesus, God floods us with His grace and removes all sin-guilt. The natural result of this divine forgiveness is gratitude for all God has done for us. For many, there is great emotion involved in the beginning of our relationship with God as well as during different seasons of our spiritual journey. Yet, loving God isn't based simply on emotion. Out of our gratitude for who God is and what He has done in our lives, the natural result is a desire to honor Him, please Him, and follow His direction and guidance. This is the type of obedience Jesus is calling for.

- **Love your neighbor = Love everyone.**

Jesus continues by saying that the second greatest command is to *"Love your neighbor as yourself." (Matthew 22:39 – NIV)* You probably already know your "neighbor" is actually every person in the world not just the people who live on your right and left – and not just the people who are easy to like. Jesus is calling us to love the people in our world as we continue loving ourselves and as much as we love ourselves.

You love yourself, don't you? If you didn't, you wouldn't spend so much time eating (to sustain your body), picking out an outfit (to look just right), or spending massive amounts of money to cut and style your hair (oftentimes to impress the opposite sex).

We love ourselves, and we should!

God created every one of us with incredible gifts, talents, and qualities, and each of us on this planet has inherent value. That's why Jesus calls us to love every single person. It's not because of their appearance or behavior. Nor is it on account of their ethnicity, education, or social standing.

We love our neighbor for one reason - because God created them.

This includes the high-caste Hindus who didn't want us to open a school for the Dalit children who wouldn't have had an education otherwise, and it means that I choose to love my Muslim neighbors even though I'm confused by some of their politics.

Ultimately, God calls me to love people with dignity, respect, and honor regardless of how much they're like me or whether they even believe like I do. Why? Because God not only created them, but He loves them.

- **Go and make disciples = Help people follow Jesus with you.**

  As we receive God's grace, we become a conduit of His love. One of the most beautiful ways we can love someone is by introducing him or her to Jesus.

  After resurrecting from the dead, Jesus meets his disciples on a mountain in Galilee and says to them, *"All authority in heaven and on earth has been given to me. Therefore go and make disciples of all nations, baptizing them in the name of the Father and of the Son and of the Holy Spirit, and teaching them to obey everything I have commanded you. And surely I am with you always, to the very end of the age." (Matthew 28:18-20 – NIV)*

  This commission wasn't just for the 11 disciples who were standing in front of Him. This message is for you and me. The Apostle Paul calls us *"ambassadors for Christ"* and *"ministers of reconciliation"* – sent out on a mission to love people and invite them to accept God's free gift of salvation by following Jesus.

As I travel the Western world, it seems like Christians focus more on "evangelism" than Jesus' call to make disciples, and this emphasis tends to go in one of two directions. At one extreme, some hold bright yellow and black signs outside of public sporting events with Scriptures emblazoned across them. While large numbers of other Christians shrink back from telling anyone about Jesus in order to distance themselves from the first extremists.

God's vision for us as His children is to help others follow in the footsteps of Jesus as we are doing the same. That's not just a one-time event (as in the case of holding up a sign), and it's more than just "letting our light shine" (without speaking any words).

If you haven't caught on to the theme quite yet, God's vision is all about people. Every aspect of God's general vision for our lives is for the ultimate benefit of humankind. His vision has always been about people, because He created us and loves us.

Not only does He want us to respond to His love by loving him back through obedience, but He also wants us to love our fellow human beings. And, ultimately, as we follow Jesus, he calls us to help others follow Him as well.

In general, God's vision for our lives is completely and utterly focused on men, women, and children - humankind.

Resisting Clarity

She turned and zigzags her way in the direction of a mud hut, and I told Gideon, my manager, to follow after her. As I rushed toward my scheduled meeting, he ended up connecting with her daughter and offering to pay for the cataract surgery. To his surprise, the elderly woman initially resisted the idea. Not only was she scared of the procedure, but she didn't think it would even work on her. On top of that, she thought we were tricking her into owing us some money.

With her daughter's convincing, the woman finally allowed Gideon to arrange for transportation to a local clinic the following week where we had scheduled a full day of cataract surgeries – all free of charge for elderly men and women we minister to.

On the day after the surgeries, we bring all the patients to our campus for the doctor to remove their bandages and check their eyes. I immediately recognize the woman from the side of the road, and I embrace her with both arms even though she can't see me with her eyes covered up.

Patients are given sunglasses to protect their eyes after surgery.

"It is so good to see you, my dear. I'm the one who saw you on the side of the road last week. Do you remember?"

"Ah, yes. Well, I still can't see you," she jokes as she gestures to the white bandages taped over her eyes.

"You'll be able to see soon, and I want to be the first person you look at."

One by one, the doctor slowly removes the tape from each patient's eyes. Every person is examined and given a pair of sunglasses to protect their eyes during the healing process. Some see clearly as the bandages come off –

while others take a week or two to recover clarity.

As I stand behind the doctor, he starts to pull the gauze, and her already wrinkly face begins to scrunch up as the tape stretches her skin. Her eyes begin to blink open and closed several times as she seems to focus in my direction. What was once a sullen face quickly turns into the brightest smile you can imagine.

"I can see! I can see!" she kept exclaiming. "I'd forgotten what it's like to see clearly!"

These moments make it worth it all. Sometimes, Jesus brings sight to the blind through miraculous prayers, and other times He does it through the hands of a skilled doctor. Either way, I'm thankful.

You better believe clarity changed that woman's life.

Because of her poor eyesight, she quit cooking years ago, since it was just too dangerous. She was unable to walk across the street through busy traffic to go to the market. And, she never went anywhere after dark, because it was impossible to see anything at all.

Remember how she had been resistant to the procedure in the beginning? I don't think we're that much different when it comes to gaining clarity on God's vision for our lives, and here are some reasons why:

1. **We have a hard time seeing beyond our current circumstances.**

   I don't know what's going on in your life right now. My guess is there are some good parts and some tough parts. You know why? Because that's true for almost all of us. The challenge comes in being willing to look beyond our outward situation (both the good and not so good) and remain open to what God envisions for us.

   As my Mom began her ministry, there were two women, named Samedanamma and Marayama, who followed her around from village to village praying passionately for everyone they came across. They had quite a gift for sharing messages with people that seemed to come straight from God – words of wisdom, divine insight into a person's situation, or even prophetic pronouncements about God's plans for someone's future.

In one instance when I was 15 years old, they began to pray over my Mom and spoke these words (seemingly on God's behalf), "My daughter, I have seen your tears. I have seen your heart and passion and burden. I have a plan for your children – to use them to take the Gospel to the nations. Many people will be blessed as I use them all around the world."

From that point on, these two women would lay their hands on me anytime I was within arms length, "My son. I have a plan to use you for God's glory. You will be traveling around the world."

Did they not realize I was living in an orphanage? Had they not seen my life? These two women were talking about me flying around the globe, and I didn't even have enough money to take the bus across town. They were saying I was going to feed thousands of people, and I wasn't even sure if I was going to eat the next week. I shook it off as nothing more than them saying something nice to my Mom in order to get a free meal after the church service.

"God, you said that you are going to use my children and send them to the nations," my Mom would pray regularly. "You are a good God!"

Out of respect for my Mom, I never spoke negatively about these so-called prophecies. She kept believing God that this promise would come true, but I just thought she was a bit crazy. Little did I know God was trying to give me clarity and direction for my life, but I couldn't see beyond my outward circumstances. I was too focused on my own immediate challenges that I couldn't imagine God's future blessings.

What is it about your current situation that clouds your ability to believe God has an incredible vision for your life?

2. We don't believe God could use someone like us.

When I left to attend a Bible college in Bangalore, I knew that I wanted to serve God and this preparation was part of the process. My underwater calling was now taking me 10 hours away from my small hometown of Tenali to a bustling metropolis with a different culture all its own.
Because students were attending from different Indian states (with their own language or dialect) and even from other countries, English was the language of choice. Unfortunately, I was still trying to figure out what

my classmates meant by "let's ketchup later", and I was a long way from figuring out the usage of affect versus effect.

Let's just say I was a long way from home.

My friend and I at Southern Asia Bible College

I became so distraught one afternoon that I packed my bags, and I hid them in my room in preparation to leave the next day. I kept asking myself, "Why am I here? How could God use me? I'm just a simple boy from Tenali."

Without knowing my plans to leave, a friend invited me to go to a meeting that evening to hear Pastor Prabhakar.

After traveling over one hour to reach the location, we arrived to see hundreds of people already standing in line to get into the church – including many who were sick or unable to walk. During the service, I was amazed to see this pastor expressing such faith and extending his hand to touch those in need. People were miraculously being healed and jumping for joy as God touched them in powerful ways.

After the service, my friend introduced me to Pastor Prabhakar, and he invited me into a small prayer room at the church. Without having knowledge of my situation, he began to pray for me and speak on behalf of God into my life. "My son, I have a plan. You are here for a purpose. I know you are frustrated and don't want to stay, but, My son this is the place. I'm going to guide you and teach you many things. I'm going to pour out My knowledge on you. You're going to be a giant in the Kingdom of God, and I'm going to use you in many nations."

As soon as he uttered the word "nations", I checked out and couldn't help but think of those two crazy women following my Mom around. "Here we go again," I thought to myself.

I walked away feeling somewhat hopeful, but I still wasn't 100 percent sure God could use me in the midst of my limitations or even wanted me to stay at the college.

Isn't it funny how others can sometimes see God's vision for our lives so clearly, but the message comes in blurry for us because of our own insecurities?

3. We're more comfortable with what's already known.

The words of Pastor Prabhakar echoed in my mind as I fell asleep that night, but I woke up with more questions than answers.

"What did he mean by 'pour out My knowledge on you'? Doesn't that mean God's going to supernaturally fill me with all the stuff I am learning here at Bible college? Maybe God just wants me to go back home."

In all reality, I was the one who wanted to go back home. It's easy to superimpose what's most comfortable for us over the top of what God's been whispering in our ears. It's a natural tendency within all of us to move toward what is already familiar and avoid things that are stretching and different. We gravitate to that which is known.

I knew what life was like in Tenali, but everything about my experience in Bangalore (the language, the culture, the people) was uncharted territory. The pull of the "known" was so strong that I was willing to avoid the clarity of God's vision for my life.

Two days after my prayer session with the pastor, I grabbed my bags and shut the door of my dorm room behind me. Since I didn't have the 150 rupees to get back home, I stopped by the office of a faculty member, Jacob Charian, to ask for help.

"Sir, could you please give me 150 rupees? I need to go back home." I said.

"What is wrong? Is there something wrong with your mother? Is she ill?" he asked, as if he couldn't see through my freshman worry.

"No...I...I just don't want to stay here anymore. Everything is so different here, and I just don't think I can handle it."

Without saying a word, he opened his well-worn Bible and began to read, *"For God has not given us a spirit of fear, but of power and of love and of a sound mind." (2 Timothy 1:7 – NKJV)*

As he placed the Scriptures back on the table, Professor Charian looked me in the eyes. "Suresh, God has not brought you all the way here to give up. We haven't been called to simply 'begin', but we're here to 'complete'. Why are you worrying about the unknowns of the future? God has a destiny for you, and this is the place where He has called you to learn at His feet. I'm challenging you today. You can do much better. Do not leave. Stay and allow God to complete the work that He has begun within you. Stay a few more days. If you're still unhappy, I'll give you the money to go home."

That which is familiar has a way of scrambling the incoming signal containing God's vision for our lives. My guess is that you've had moments when you sensed God was calling you to courageously step out in faith, but the pull of the 'known' reigned you back in.

> It's not uncommon to start asking questions that begin with "what if" to ward off what God may be calling us to do.

That morning, I left my professor's office and went back to my dorm room with an incredible sense of confidence, hope, and a renewed spirit. I started thinking about the clear message interwoven through each one of these encounters. From the prophecies of Samedanamma and Marayama to the prayer of Pastor Prabhakar to the challenging words from Professor Charian, God was making it clear He had a unique and specific vision for my life.

Over the next month, I started learning English much more quickly, and I became accustomed with life in the big city. More than anything, I sensed Jesus' presence in a powerful way, and God's vision was starting to come into focus.

After three years in Bangalore, I graduated, moved back to Tenali, and joined my Mom's ministry – what was then called Evangelical Association for Revival Education (EARE). I focused on evangelism, while my brother, Sudheer, oversaw administration. If I would have returned home during that first month of Bible college, I may have missed out on God's vision for my life.

Me, my Mom, and my brother Sudheer

You could be asking yourself, "Why am I here?" Why am I at this school? Why am I in this job? Why am I in this marriage? What is my future?"

Perhaps, you feel stuck, alone, or empty. Maybe, your future looks like a zero! I'm telling you that God has a vision for your life. As if His 'general' vision wasn't enough, I actually believe He has a 'specific' calling for you as an individual.

How to Get Clear About God's Vision For You

For many of us, the process of discovering God's unique calling on our lives can feel unbelievably daunting, but I want to invite you to reframe it as a spiritual adventure. Rather than worrying about getting it exactly right or possibly missing out on something, listen to the words of Jesus as He continues to whisper, "Follow me." These two words weren't just uttered once when you first chose to accept Him. He continues to nudge you to walk beside Him as He leads you on the adventure of being His ambassador in this world.

1. **Ask God, "What do you want me to do with my life?"**

   The fact that you would start by asking God the question may seem obvious, but many of us skip this critical step. Our God is a speaking God, and He knows what's best for each one of us. How do you sense He wants to use you to serve people in this season of your life? (Remember, people are His central focus.)

2. **Ask yourself, "What need or issue captures my heart?"**

   When you see a need and your heart wells up with compassion...
   When you witness injustice and you become angry...
   When you lay awake at night concerned about someone...
   That's a signal that God has a vision and purpose to use you in that situation.

3. **Ask others, "What talents do I have to invest?"**

   If you can't see how you can be used to make a difference with an issue that's captured your heart, ask a friend or family member. Sometimes, what is cloudy to us can be incredibly clear in the eyes of others. Ask someone you trust to help you discern ways that you can use your gifts to bring help and hope to whoever is in need.

4. **Ask someone in need, "How can I help?"**

   If you see someone in need, don't stand around waiting for someone to ask for your help. Reach out to that person or organization and offer your assistance. God may use them to help clarify His vision for your life.

The Bible is chock-full of people who God used for a specific purpose. Don't get hung up on your current circumstances or your perceived lack of __________ (fill in the blank) or even your fear of the unknown. God has a great plan for you and your future. In fact, let's take a few minutes to look at some examples from the Bible that demonstrate this truth:

- **Be encouraged even if you feel lost.**

  If you're still feeling a bit fuzzy (or even dejected), let me remind you of the words found in Jeremiah 29:11. While it may be tempting to quote this passage in an effort to gain emotional comfort, I find even greater empowerment in understanding the actual biblical context.

  These words were spoken to Jews living in the urban city of Babylon - people whose nation had been humiliated in war. People who had been torn from their homeland and felt alone, out-of-place, and alienated. These were people who didn't want to be where they were.

  "This is what the Lord says: "When seventy years are completed for Babylon, I will come to you and fulfill my good promise to bring you back to this place. For I know the plans I have for you," declares the Lord, "plans to prosper you and not to harm you, plans to give you hope and a future. Then you will call on me and come and pray to me, and I will listen to you. You will seek me and find me when you seek me with all your heart. I will be found by you," declares the Lord, "and will bring you back from captivity." (Jeremiah 29:10-13 – NIV)

  What an incredible promise to the people of Israel who were inevitably feeling lost in a foreign country. God was going to bring them back!

  If you feel cloudy or confused, this is message is true for you as well. God does know His plans for you, and they are plans to prosper you and not to harm you, plans that include a wonderful future.

- **Don't be surprised by opposition.**

  While Jesus has plans to give you a full life, we have an enemy that seeks to thwart God's vision coming to fruition through you. Therefore, don't be surprised when opposition appears.

BY GOD'S VISION FOR MY LIFE

In 1 Corinthians 16, we read about Paul's plans to visit followers of Jesus in the city of Corinth, *"After I go through Macedonia, I will come to you...I hope to spend some time with you, if the Lord permits. But I will stay on at Ephesus until Pentecost, because a great door for effective work has opened to me, and there are many who oppose me." (1 Corinthians 16:5-9 – NIV)*

Notice that Paul says a "great door for effective work" has opened up for him. In other words, he is clear about God's vision, and he's focused on doing his part. Yet, he also says, "there are many who oppose me." That's all he says. In the following verses, he doesn't even mention it again. It's like it's just a fact to him – nothing to discuss or go on and on about.

Why are we so surprised that challenges, distractions, and hurdles come our way when we start to gain clarity about how God wants to use us in this world? Rather than getting hung up on the opposition, let me ask you, what "great door for effective work" has God opened for you? Focus on that instead!

- **Don't miss out on the opportunity right in front of you.**

The truth is God is bringing many people into your life. God is nudging you to do something in your neighborhood. He is asking you to meet the needs of the vulnerable and broken who live in your community. He is calling you to respond to the vision He has placed in your heart.

Unfortunately, our addiction to busyness and love for the accumulation of material possessions blurs our vision, and we walk right by the very people God is calling us to help.

It's like what we see in Acts 3 with the man in front of the temple gate: *"Now a man who was lame from birth was being carried to the temple gate called Beautiful, where he was put every day to beg from those going into the temple courts." (Acts 3:2 – NIV)*

Think about it. How many people passed him by every day? Maybe a few people dropped a coin or two in his cup to appease their guilt, but most people walked right on by. Thousands of people were blind to the man's true need.

Yet, when Peter and John were going into the temple, they stopped. Why? Because they were clear about their purpose, and they were willing to obey God in the moment. They were confident in what they had to give, and it wasn't silver or gold. It was power from Jesus.

Oftentimes, we're asking God to provide a miracle while He's asking us to use the supernatural power He's already instilled within us.
We pray, "God, come and heal our nation with all these problems!"

He says, "I've given you gifts, talents, financial resources, and the power of the Holy Spirit. What are you waiting for?"

Yes, we should pray, but God has uniquely equipped every one of us to take action. You may not be able to eliminate the entire problem, but you can make a difference. You have resources, and God is calling you to leverage them on behalf of people in need.

Will you be compelled by God's vision for your life?

SMALL GROUP WEEK #3

Getting Started

1. What did you "see" this week that inspired you? Was it God's creation, an interaction at work, a video online? What was it? How did it inspire you?

2. Solomon tells us that without vision, people perish. Do you think a "vision" for our lives is important? Why or why not?

Going Deeper

3. Read these three passages on your own, and then pick three different people to read them at the small group:

   a. Matthew 22:34-40
   b. John 14:23-24
   c. Matthew 28:16-20

4. Suresh writes that God's "general vision" for our lives is to:

   a. Love God (which equals "obey God.")
   b. Love your neighbor (which equals "love everyone.")
   c. Go and make disciples (which equals "help people follow Jesus with you.")

Do you think this is what God envisions for our lives? Why or why not?

5. We read, "God's vision for our lives is completely and utterly focused on men, women, and children - humankind." Why do you think God wants us to be focused on helping people?

6. Out of the three reasons why we resist God's vision for our lives, which one do you think most people struggle with?

   a. Have a hard time seeing beyond our current circumstances.
   b. Don't believe God could use someone like us.
   c. More comfortable with what's already known.

Applying It To Your Life

7. Have you asked God recently, "What do you want me to do with my life?" What have you sensed Him saying?

8. What need or issue in our world captures your heart? Could that be a sign to you?

9. What gifts and talents could you invest to help humanity? What's holding you back?

10. Based on what we've discussed today, how do think you're supposed to respond this week?

CHAPTER 4

I AM COMPELLED BY AN UTTER DEPENDENCE ON GOD

In 2004, I flew to Canada to visit our ministry's supporters there for the first time. As you can imagine, sleeping can be quite a challenge when there's a 12-hour time difference from what you're used to. What is 12noon back at home is the middle of the night in North America, and the result is often odd sleeping patterns and intense dreams.

As I crawl into bed exhausted at my host home, I can't help but pray for our ministry back in India, my family, and of course, my mother. After falling asleep, I begin to experience a dream that felt as real as everyday life.

In what ultimately became a nightmare, my Mom suddenly dies, and all my family is crying hysterically. We lay my Mom's dead body on the ground in front of our home as we mourn her passing (which is customary in India), and my head drapes over her chest as I weep.

The shock of this dream jolts me out of a deep sleep, and I immediately sit upright in bed glancing at the clock - 12midnight. I pick up my cellphone and dial my Mom. The few seconds of ringing feel like an eternity.

My wife, Christina, picks up the phone, and I ask, "How is Mom doing?" trying not to sound worried. She is fine. Nothing is wrong. She is going about her daily business of running the ministry. In fact, my Mom gets on the phone, and we chat for a few minutes – giving updates back and forth.

I don't say a word about the dream – to anyone.

Five days later (still in Canada), I have the exact same dream again. I wake up crying and roll out of bed kneeling on the hardwood bedroom floor. I am convinced something dreadful is going to happen.

"God, please don't let my Mom die," I cry out over and over as tears stream down my face.

After finishing my visit in Canada, I board a plane to head to Phoenix, Arizona, for more meetings. Before the flight attendants can even start giving the preflight safety instructions, I sense God speaking to me, "My son, I am preparing your heart. I am going to take my servant home."

There is nothing I can do in that moment but pray…and trust…and utterly depend on God. If Jesus is truly worthy of my trust, I knew that I had to put my confidence in Him – knowing that He has a plan and purpose for this very moment. During the entire flight from Canada, I keep hearing the same thing over and over, "Prepare your heart. Prepare your heart."

After retrieving my luggage, I flag down a taxi and step into the air-conditioned car – continuing to sweat out of fear and pain in my heart. As soon as we arrive at the hotel, I head straight to the front desk and ask for the Wi-Fi password to check my email. With my laptop sitting on the hotel's counter, my eyes scan through the incoming emails to catch the two-word subject line – "Lalitha died."

Believe it or not, in that moment, there is no pain. There is no crying. God had been preparing me for the past 10 days. He knows that I am so close to my mother I would have had a heart attack without His divine preparation. Instantly, I call the pastor I was to be visiting with in Phoenix, and I tell him I need to fly home.

In 2004, my Mom died at the age of 66 after investing her life in over 40 years of ministry among the least, last, and lost of India. More than 3,000 people attended her funeral to celebrate her life and give glory to God.

BY AN UTTER DEPENDENCE ON GOD

As the older son, I immediately picked up the mantle of the ministry. When she died, we had a network of over 300 churches and 100 orphans living in our children's homes.

I was completely overwhelmed.

Although I had been working alongside my Mom for quite a few years, I never imagined doing this without her. She was the heart and soul of our ministry.

As Jesus was preparing his disciples for His own death, He warned them, *"Most assuredly, I say to you, unless a grain of wheat falls into the ground and dies, it remains alone; but if it dies, it produces much grain." (John 12-24 – NKJV)*

In the same way, I had a sense that God was going to use my Mom's death to produce incredible fruit in our ministry. It wasn't that she was holding us back in some way, but I knew we were entering into a new season. I believe her prayers were finally coming to fruition. People throughout India and even all over the world were emailing me with heartfelt condolences and prophetic words of encouragement. Many discerned a shift in the spiritual realm - and that we were entering a new season of ministry.

In the days after my Mom's passing, I was drawn to the story of Moses and Joshua. For 40 years, Moses had been leading the children of Israel throughout the desert in preparation to enter the Promised Land. Yet, once Moses died, there was a shift in the spiritual realm.

"After the death of Moses the servant of the LORD, the LORD said to Joshua son of Nun, Moses' aide: "Moses my servant is dead. Now then, you and all these people, get ready to cross the Jordan River into the land I am about to give to them—to the Israelites. I will give you every place where you set your foot, as I promised Moses. Your territory will extend from the desert to Lebanon, and from the great river, the Euphrates—all the Hittite country—to the Mediterranean Sea in the west. No one will be able to stand against you all the days of your life. As I was with Moses, so I will be with you; I will never leave you nor forsake you. Be strong and courageous, because you will lead these people to inherit the land I swore to their ancestors to give them." (Joshua 1:1-6 – NIV)

While I have no intention of comparing my Mom to Moses or me to Joshua, I did take courage in the fact that God will never leave me nor forsake me. I also sensed we were about ready to enter into something my Mom had been praying for – but not yet experienced.

I will tell you that God began to miraculously expand our territory. There is no other explanation for the incredible growth and favor we received as a ministry in the years to come.

My Mom's legacy can be seen in the lives of countless people throughout our ministry today. From pastors in remote villages who were just children when she invested in them to women who are overseeing our growing network of children's homes, Lalitha Kumari's fingerprints are all over the work. Although she cast a huge vision many years ago, I'm not even sure she could imagine what God is now doing through her humble beginnings.

To date, Harvest India has over 1,600 churches, 28 children's homes with 1,300 orphans, 12 Bible schools, eight elderly homes, an HIV/AIDS hospice, a hospital with 50 beds, a leprosy ministry and housing project, eight nursing schools, two junior colleges, one degree college, and more than 400 water wells have been given to Dalit villages.

As we stand on the firm ground of my Mom's legacy, the only possible way for all this to happen is through our utter dependence on God. There is no other way.

Jesus tells us, *"I am the vine; you are the branches. If you remain in me and I in you, you will bear much fruit; apart from me you can do nothing." (John 15:5 – NIV)*

While it can be tempting to believe these incredible statistics are simply the result of my ingenuous leadership skills and the hard work of our team, I'm well aware we couldn't do any of this without Jesus as the Source. He knows the needs of the people, and He has the solutions. We are His mere vessels – His representatives – who go about doing His work as He leads and guides. Without Him, our work would amount to nothing. It would be short-lived and never stand the test of time.

Not only does Paul challenge us to build our lives (and ministry) on the foundation of Jesus Christ, but he also says our works will ultimately be judged on quality. *"If anyone builds on this foundation using gold, silver, costly stones, wood, hay or straw, their work will be shown for what it is, because the Day will bring it to light. It will be revealed with fire, and the fire will test the quality of each person's work. If what has been built survives, the builder will receive a reward. If it is burned up, the builder will suffer loss but yet will be saved—even though only as one escaping through the flames." (1 Corinthians 3:12-15 – NIV)*

He indicates that on the Day of Judgment the work of our lives will be tested by fire. If we have depended on God as our Source and built a life that honors Him and serves humanity, our work will survive, and we will receive a reward. To be clear, this isn't tied to our salvation or even His unconditional love for us. Yet, it is a clear message God wants us to invest our time, talent, and treasure in a way that's for the benefit of others – not just ourselves.

If you want to do something incredible with your life, may I suggest that you develop an utter dependence on God?

Self-Sufficient or God Dependent?

When I visit the US, UK, or Canada and spend time among fellow Christians, I'm shocked at the lack of God-dependent prayer. Sure, most people feel obligated to pray (especially in my presence) before meals or at the beginning of a gathering. I'm talking about prayer as a regular part of a Jesus-follower's life – the primary way we remain connected to the vine and embrace our dependence upon Him.

At first glance, there doesn't seem to be much that Western Christians are lacking. While there are exceptions, I find that most people in the West are generally more self-sufficient than God-dependent.

Of course, I'm just an outsider looking in and may have things all wrong. You tell me.

With all the resources of education, technology, healthcare, money, and modern transportation, my sense is that most Christians have little need to depend on God. You can simply take out a loan, put it on credit card, search for it on Google, go to the doctor, or take an airplane to a faraway city for a relaxing vacation. Yes, these modern conveniences have made life better in most cases, but it's easy to think that a reliance on God is simply for the weak or needy.

COMPELLED

It's not until tragedy strikes that we realize how powerless we truly are.

Whether it's a natural disaster that hits close to home or a devastating car accident or even a diagnosis of cancer, all of a sudden we're faced with the reality of our own frailty. In those moments, all the money and technology in the world pales in comparison to the unlimited resources of our Heavenly Father.

Unfortunately, our material excess can blind us to the fact we are in need. We can go to church week after week and never be dependent on God. We can read the Bible day after day and never recognize our need for the One who created us and sustains us with every living breath.

There are two attitudes of the heart preventing us from being dependent:

- **Self-sufficiency – "I can do it on my own."**

  When we live in such a way that we don't think we need God's help, we've moved from a healthy sense of confidence rooted in our identity in Christ to an unhealthy belief that we can do everything on our own. You may never say, "I don't need God's help," but is your life evidence of that attitude?

  The antidote is to cultivate an awareness of our need and acknowledge God's faithfulness. David writes, *"Your love, Lord, reaches to the heavens, your faithfulness to the skies." (Psalm 36:5 – NIV)* In the same way that our needs are never-ending, so is God's love and faithfulness.

- **Self-centeredness – "I did it on my own."**

  When we look back at our accomplishments – whether it be finishing our education, getting a job promotion, healing from an illness, or just making it through a challenging week – and think we did it on our own, our attitude is egotistical and absorbed.

  The Bible is telling us, *"But remember the Lord your God, for it is he who gives you the ability to produce wealth..." (Deuteronomy 8:18 – NIV)* It is He who gives you and me the ability to do anything and everything – including breathe. Let us not take His abundant gifts for granted, and let's continually express our gratitude for all His blessings.

BY AN UTTER DEPENDENCE ON GOD

Other than when my Mom passed away, there has been no other time I sensed a greater dependence on God than when Christina and I were trying to have children.

After getting married, it's normal for Indian couples to immediately seek to have children. In fact, most get pregnant within the year after their wedding day. Month after month after month, Christina isn't becoming pregnant, and we are becoming worried. Neighbors and friends continue to ask, "Any good news?" and we are embarrassed and heartbroken.

After three years, we finally go see a doctor, and they indicate we may never have children. That was a miserable day, but we remain confident in God. We never give up, and we have a faith and a hope that God can do anything. We pray and cry and pray some more.

I know what it's like to not hear the answer your heart desires.

One day during a church service, a friend of ours was praying for Christina and me, and they begin to speak a message on behalf of God. "My daughter, fear not. You are going to have a baby within the next year. I'm going to honor your prayers, and I'm going to give you a boy. Your tears are in the palm of my hand, and I'm going to bless you. You can count the date from this very month."

Because of our deep dependence on God, we receive it as if it was truth. We start looking and waiting. 12 days afterward, my wife starts to feel sick in the morning for a couple of days in a row, so we head to the doctor again. They confirm the great news. We are pregnant! Thank you, Jesus.

Nine months later, our son, David, is born, and now God has also blessed us with Mercy and Nancy. There were literally years when we wondered if we would ever have any children, and now we have the three most amazing children in the world (but I may be a bit biased).

In those dark times, I was driven to my knees in prayer continually acknowledging my dependence on God. Without God, I can't imagine what I would have done. In similar circumstances, many turn to every conceivable form of self-medication imaginable – overeating, overspending, alcohol, drugs, and sexual promiscuity. The hope is that one of these things will soothe the pain and brokenness, but only Jesus can truly provide the Hope we long for.

That's why I'm compelled to remain in a posture of utter dependence – because I am dependent upon Him. He is my only Source of life, and I can do nothing without Him. The more I embrace this reality, the more confidence I can have in his vision and plan for my life. And, ultimately, the more peace and joy I can experience through the inevitable ups and the downs.

The Path of Dependency

While dependency on God is an attitude of the heart, the path by which it is embraced is through prayer. I've never known another person who valued daily communication with God more than my mother, and she instilled its importance within me as well.

From an early age, my Mom began praying with me and teaching me that I could talk to God and ask Him for help in my own life. In fact, she believed prayer was as important as breathing or eating – things no one in their right mind would ever stop doing.

I vividly remember a time when I was around five years old when I woke up from a night's sleep and walked into the kitchen where my Mom was preparing breakfast.

She asked, "Son, did you pray?"

I looked away from her – not wanting to respond.

"Tell me. Look at my face," she insisted. "Back to your room and go pray."

That may feel legalistic or harsh to you, but for us as Christians living in India, it is a realization that God is the Source of everything. Most of us don't have the luxury of relying on government welfare, using credit cards as a backup, or even depending on the electricity to stay on all day.

My Mom was training me to rely on my God to meet all my needs.

Because of her maturity, she knew something I didn't yet know. It wasn't about praying a certain amount of time or with just the right words. It was about cultivating an attitude trust and obedience. While it may have been uncomfortable in the moment, she trusted that I would ultimately experience what she experienced.

And, she was right. Until you taste a deep dependence on God through prayer, you won't know what it's like.

For quite a few years, Harvest India rented a large building that housed our Bible college, ministry office, medical center, and a church, but the owner of the building eventually agreed to sell it to us for $50,000 if we paid the entire amount within one year.

Our original facility

As we shared the vision with our partners in the West, they were incredibly generous, and we started making large payments on the facility. Because we weren't able to pay the full amount within the first year, the owner ended up extending the agreement for another 12 months. At the end of the second year, we had only paid $42,000, and we simply couldn't come up with another $8,000.

After arriving at the owner's home to share the bad news, he informed us that he was no longer willing to sell the building at the same price since it had doubled in value. Now, he wanted $100,000! Understanding our situation, he was willing to give us the $42,000 back.

COMPELLED

After two years of raising money and thinking we were going to own our first facility, my heart was crushed. What was I going to tell the donors in the United States?

Christina kept telling me, "God has a good plan, and He will open new doors. We just need to pray."

Three days later, a different landowner named Venkataswrlu contacted our team, because he heard we were looking for a facility. "I have 20 acres of land, and I need $50,000 for my daughter's dowry."

I immediately rushed to the property, and I loved the land – only 15 minutes away from the other facility.

"How much money do you have now?" he asked.

"I have $42,000," I said hesitantly.

"Okay, I will take it."

Little did he know, the money was in huge rice bag underneath our bed, and I hadn't slept for three days because I was crying out to God in prayer. The landowner came over to our home, and I opened the bag to reveal a huge pile of cash. He was shocked to see all that money.

If Jesus took regular time to pray, why aren't we doing the same? He Himself depended on God the Father for wisdom and power.

In fact, Jesus told a group of Jewish leaders, *"Very truly I tell you, the Son can do nothing by himself; he can do only what he sees his Father doing, because whatever the Father does the Son also does. For the Father loves the Son and shows him all he does. Yes, and he will show him even greater works than these, so that you will be amazed." (John 5:19-20 – NIV)*

How does Jesus know what the Father wants Him to do? Jesus asks Him, and He depended on God the Father for direction.

What a privilege it is to have access to the Creator of the universe who is the Source of everything we could ever need or desire in this life!

BY AN UTTER DEPENDENCE ON GOD

I've already shared with you how my wife and I pray every morning after waking up – praising God, confessing our sins, and asking for His help in every aspect of our lives. Some people write down their prayers in a journal and others quietly allow the words to simply flow from their minds, but I'm more of an old-fashioned, cry out to God, pray out loud kind of guy. For me, there's something about verbalizing the words in the same way I would talk to a friend or even cry out for help when I'm in need.

While "not knowing how" may be the excuse some Christians give, I think the real reasons are mostly centered on self-sufficiency and busyness. Because I strongly believe that embracing our dependence on God is directly connected to the fruit our lives will bear, I want to share the reasons why I pray:

1. **Prayer reminds me who God is and what He has done.**

   When I begin my times of prayer, I call out as many character qualities of God I can think of, and I often connect a Scripture to that quality.

   "God, you are my Creator. You created the entire universe, and I thank you. I praise you for your holiness. You are set apart, and I remember how you displayed that to Moses when you asked him to take off his sandals because the place he was standing was holy ground."

   By connecting God's attributes with examples in Scripture, I'm solidifying this knowledge within me. Then, I'll oftentimes recount how I have personally experienced that particular character quality of God in my own life.

   I love what the writer of the Psalms says, *"I will remember the deeds of the Lord; yes, I will remember your miracles of long ago. I will consider all your works and meditate on all your mighty deeds." (Psalms 77:11-12 – NIV)*

   We are enjoying the blessing, but we forget to recognize the Source of the blessings.

2. **Prayer cultivates humility within my life.**

   By talking to God at the beginning of my day, I'm choosing to center my life on Him – rather than on myself. Essentially, I am saying, "You are

God, and I am not. You created this entire world, and I just live in it."

Humility is an honest assessment of who I am and what I bring to the table of life. As I talk with God, I'm taking my rightful place as the creation and reminding myself that He is the Creator.

Peter writes, *"Humble yourselves, therefore, under God's mighty hand, that he may lift you up in due time. Cast all your anxiety on him because he cares for you." (1 Peter 5:6-7 – NIV)*

As much I would like to be in control of all aspects of my life, I'm not. By taking time to talk to God, I'm acknowledging that I need Him, and He will lift me up.

3. Prayer helps me maintain continuity in my relationship with God.

The Scriptures tell me that God will never leave me nor forsake me, but I do realize that the quality of my relationship with Him is impacted by my willingness to connect through prayer. In the same way my marriage would be impacted by multiple days (or even weeks) of silence between my wife and I, the continuity of my close connection with God is affected as well. Will God leave me? Never! Will my own sense of daily intimacy wane? Probably so.

Paul writes, *"Rejoice always, pray without ceasing, in everything give thanks; for this is the will of God in Christ Jesus for you." (1 Thessalonians 5:16-18 – NIV)*

I believe that Paul is encouraging us to remain continuously connected to God – cultivating an intimacy by finding our joy in Him, talking with Him, and expressing our thanks to Him.

4. Prayer recharges my spiritual batteries.

With all that you and I have going on in this world, we need more than coffee and chai to keep us going. Our world can offer material possessions, but it can never offer the peace, joy, and hope we need to persevere through life's challenges.

As my friend likes to say, "You can buy a mattress, but you can't buy sleep."

In other words, the peace that allows us to sleep at night can't be purchased with the money of this world. It only comes through having our spiritual batteries recharged through prayer.

David tells us to, *"Taste and see that the Lord is good; blessed is the one who takes refuge in him." (Psalm 34:8-9 – NIV)*

Put your trust in Him, because He is good.

5. **Prayer changes things in my life.**

For many of us, prayer is primarily associated with getting God to do something for us – to bring about change in a challenging or painful situation. That's why I put this one last. We "get" the concept that God has the power to bring about transformation. Ironically, we seem to use Him as a last resort when things really start to go sideways in life, but I've found that talking to Him along the way seems to be a better strategy.

James, the brother of Jesus, writes, *"Is anyone among you in trouble? Let them pray. Is anyone happy? Let them sing songs of praise. Is anyone among you sick? Let them call the elders of the church to pray over them and anoint them with oil in the name of the Lord. And the prayer offered in faith will make the sick person well; the Lord will raise them up. If they have sinned, they will be forgiven. Therefore confess your sins to each other and pray for each other so that you may be healed. The prayer of a righteous person is powerful and effective." (James 5:13-16 – NIV)*

You are that "righteous person", because you have been put in right-standing with God through the sacrifice of Jesus on the cross. Therefore, your prayer is both powerful and effective. More often than not, the first thing that prayer changes is me. When I come to God on a daily basis acknowledging my dependence on Him, there's something that shifts in my heart. I become less arrogant and more humble. I'm less impatient and more loving. My focus is less on selfish desires and more about the needs of others. And, yes, God changes things outside of me as well.

Jesus tells us, *"Ask and it will be given to you; seek and you will find; knock and the door will be opened to you. For everyone who asks receives; the one who seeks finds; and to the one who knocks, the door will be opened." (Matthew 7:7-8 – NIV)*

> I don't know why God answers some prayers with a "yes" and others with a "no" or "not yet", but I do know that He invites us to participate in the redemption of the world by talking to Him. Rather than trying to figure out the why and how behind God's decisions, I've chosen to keep trusting and asking.
>
> And, you know what? When I pray in faith, I seem to have prayers answered all the time. If I don't ask for God's help, will He still intervene? Maybe – but He's giving me the opportunity to participate in the process. Why wouldn't I take Him up on that offer?

Some people say that God is just a crutch for weak people, and I happen to agree. Think about it this way. You and I don't question why our legs hold us upright or why we rely upon them without even thinking. That's just what they are designed to do. In the same way, it is part of God's very nature to hold us up, and He has designed us in a way to depend on Him. He is dependable – able to be depended upon for all our needs.

In 2 Corinthians 12, Paul writes about an ongoing challenge in his life (thorn in his flesh) and the Lord's response to his request to take it away.

> *"But he said to me, "My grace is sufficient for you, for my power is made perfect in weakness." Therefore I will boast all the more gladly about my weaknesses, so that Christ's power may rest on me. That is why, for Christ's sake, I delight in weaknesses, in insults, in hardships, in persecutions, in difficulties. For when I am weak, then I am strong." (2 Corinthians 12:9-10 – NIV)*

Dependence may come across as weak or powerless to some, but I've chosen to live my life in light of God's divine design and His unlimited resources – not my own effort. In contrast to the power of the Holy Spirit at work within me, my feeble attempts at trying to figure things out or resolve my own problems pale in comparison to the times when I express my need for Him and ask for guidance.

It can be so tempting to live dependently only when we need something, but the truth is that we always need something. Don't we?

SMALL GROUP WEEK #4

Getting Started

1. As you think about your own life, who do you "depend on" (besides God or Jesus)?

2. Suresh wrote about how God prepared his heart for the passing of his mother. Have you ever felt like God prepared you for something? Tell us about it.

3. What do you think the difference is between self-sufficiency and self-centeredness? Look back to Suresh's description to stir your thoughts.

Going Deeper

4. Read John 15:1-8. Who is speaking these words, and what stands out to you?

5. There is a strong sense of dependence being called for in this passage. Does our culture view that trait in a positive or negative light, and why?

6. If Jesus were physically sitting with us right now, what are some practical things He would encourage us to do (and not do) in order to "remain in Him"?

Applying It To Your Life

7. If you were to ask people in your life, "What is purpose of prayer?" – what do you think they would say?

8. Suresh shares five reasons why he prays on a daily basis:

   a. Prayer reminds him who God is and what He has done.
   b. Prayer cultivates humility within his life.
   c. Prayer helps him maintain continuity in his relationship with God.
   d. Prayer recharges his spiritual batteries.
   e. Prayer changes things in his life.

   Which one of these five things do you need the most in your life?

9. Open your Bible back up to John 15. How could prayer help us live out what Jesus is calling us to in this passage?

10. This week, what would it practically look like to develop a greater dependence on God?

CHAPTER 5

I AM COMPELLED TO VALUE OTHERS ABOVE MYSELF

In the West, there is a commonly held belief you can grow up to do anything you set your sights on. Perhaps, your parents, teachers, or coaches told you to…

"Follow your dreams."
"Believe in yourself."
"Don't give up."

While millions of Western children are striving toward higher education, marrying whoever they choose, and pursuing the so-called American dream, an entire segment of the Indian population is held down under the weight of their social status as Dalits.

Rooted in the ancient Hindu caste system, Dalits or "untouchables" are a social class of people who have historically held occupations regarded as ritually impure – anything involving leatherwork, butchering, or removal of trash, animal carcasses, and waste. While opportunities have begun to open up in recent years, Dalits often work as manual laborers cleaning streets, latrines, and sewers or catching rats and snakes in the rice paddy fields.

Working in these situations is believed to pollute the individual, and this pollution is considered contagious to others. As a result, Dalits are usually segregated and banned from full participation in Hindu social life. This means they are forced to live in separate villages, attend lower quality schools, and remain outside of most temples. Opportunities for higher education and good paying jobs are severely limited, and interactions with those outside their caste are few and far between.

Imagine being thirsty on a hot day and not able to drink from a nearby water well. Envision yourself interested in someone of the opposite sex, but you know marriage isn't even a possibility because they are of a higher caste. There's no chance of getting a better job or moving to a nicer village or even providing for your children to go to a quality school.

You are stuck. You are a Dalit.
Can you imagine what that must feel like?

Dalit villages are filled with children in need.

I can. I've been that person. As a child growing up in an orphanage, our culture in India sees you as someone who has been discarded. And, as a Christian, you are regarded as a low-caste person who is weak and powerless. While discrimination based on caste has been prohibited under the Constitution of India, it still exists – especially in rural areas where we focus our work.

The reality is no one wants to go to those places. Located far away from a city or town, these areas are owned by high-caste landowners who hire poor people to work the fields – planting and harvesting year after year. The workers and their families live in nearby villages with little to no electricity, no running water, and no sewage system. When I was growing up, the workers were given food and shelter, but paid nothing else. These days, a good job working in the fields may garner up to $5 per day for a Dalit worker.

The root of all discrimination is a belief that one person (or group) is better than another based on a particular trait – skin color, ethnicity, religion, education, financial status, or anything else that may differentiate one from another.

While Hindus believe Dalits are born into their low caste based on how they lived in a previous life, the truth is the individual had no choice as to what family they would be born into. His or her birth is not a result of karma from a past existence. Instead, we believe that God has created each person with immeasurable value.

In The Message, Proverbs 22:2 says, *"The rich and the poor shake hands as equals – God made them both!"*

The Bible makes it clear that God has created every single person in His image – in the likeness of our Creator. That means that there is a godlikeness within each of us, and that is to be honored no matter what family you are born into.

Why do we respect others as equal?
Because they have the likeness of God within them.
Because God places a high value on their life.
Because God doesn't see anyone as having more worth or value.

Better Than, Less Than

While it may be easy to recognize the blatant disregard for human value among the Dalits in my country, it's a bit harder to pinpoint the subtle arrogance hidden in many of our hearts.

My guess is that you and I have a group of people we have categorized as "low caste" in our minds – probably not Dalits – perhaps people who we have deemed "less than" in some way.

We may never want to admit it to another person, but it's there. It's hidden in the recesses of our being, and it comes out in the ways we treat the people around us. Let's think for a moment about some people that may be different from us.

1. **People who look different than you.**

   Maybe it's their skin color, weight, hairstyle, clothing choice, or body modification. Do you look down on someone who is overweight? Someone who has undergone plastic surgery? Or, how about someone who wears clothes that you would deem out of style?

2. **People who speak a different language.**

   When you hear someone speaking Spanish, French, Hindi, or Korean, are you irritated? Do you automatically think they should just speak your language?

3. **People who are less (or more) educated.**

   Are you puffed up by your schooling – looking down on those who don't measure up in your eyes? Or, do you have disdain for people with more education – assuming that they look down upon you?

4. **People who live in a certain city or neighborhood.**

   When you drive by a particular neighborhood, do you wonder how someone could possibly live there? Do you lock your doors automatically thinking that one of those people might do you harm? Or, do you look down your nose at the people living in those big houses on the other side of town?

5. **People who hold different beliefs.**

   This may be the hardest one of all. What about people who are of a different religion or political party? Does your heart start pumping with anxiety when you think about them?

My guess is that you feel "better than" at least one group of people in the list above.

The result is a subtle (or not so subtle) difference in behavior toward "those people" versus individuals who happen to meet the arbitrary standard you have set in your mind. It can be as simple as avoiding contact with someone or even giving preferential treatment to another.

The Bible calls that favoritism.

Using an example of wealth and social status, James writes, *"My brothers and sisters, believers in our glorious Lord Jesus Christ must not show favoritism. Suppose a man comes into your meeting wearing a gold ring and fine clothes, and a poor man in filthy old clothes also comes in. If you show special attention to the man wearing fine clothes and say, "Here's a good seat for you," but say to the poor man, "You stand there" or "Sit on the floor by my feet," have you not discriminated among yourselves and become judges with evil thoughts?" (James 2:1-5 – NIV)*

The brother of Jesus is proposing a scenario where two men come into a place of worship, but they are treated differently based on the fact that one is rich and the other is poor.

In this case, the story illustrates that we care more about the outward appearance than what's going on inside the person. In 1 Samuel 16:7, we learn, *"The Lord does not look at the things people look at. People look at the outward appearance, but the Lord looks at the heart."* Many of us would favor the rich man over the poor man, because we believe that his wealth or power could somehow help us in ways that the poor man can't.

Let's keep reading the words of James: *"Listen, my dear brothers and sisters: Has not God chosen those who are poor in the eyes of the world to be rich in faith and to inherit the kingdom he promised those who love him? But you have dishonored the poor. Is it not the rich who are exploiting you? Are they not the ones who are dragging you into court? Are they not the ones who are blaspheming the noble name of him to whom you belong?" (James 2:5-7 – NIV)*

Isn't it interesting how we can treat the "rich" (or whatever group you prefer) more favorably than the person who is "less than"? God doesn't work that way. In fact, since great wealth is an obstacle to the kingdom of God (Matthew 19:24), there is a sense in which the poor of this world are specially blessed by Him.

Finally, James reminds the Christians that the rich are the ones who have been dragging them into court – most likely to sue them over unpaid debts and turn them into indentured servants. Essentially he's saying, "Why on Earth would you favor someone when God sees you both as equals?"

For years, I have personally witnessed how the "less than" seem to more readily accept God's gift of grace through Jesus Christ than the "better than". People in lower castes tend to recognize their spiritual needs, because it's not being masked by materialism. James says that they are "rich in faith", because they have more opportunities to trust God to meet their daily needs. Since they have no riches, they can't put their trust in them. Jesus is their only hope! That's why Jesus says, *"Blessed are the poor in spirit."*

Imitating the Humility of Jesus

Determining someone to have greater or lesser worth (and treating them in a certain way for personal gain) stems from our own selfish motives. We're either avoiding the discomfort of dealing with someone who is "less than" or wanting to gain something (usually status, power, or money) by being associated with someone who we deem is "better than." And, in thinking about our own lives, we tend to compare downward so that we end up feeling like…"Well, at least I'm better than that person."

The apostle Paul writes, *"Do nothing out of selfish ambition or vain conceit. Rather, in humility value others above yourselves, not looking to your own interests but each of you to the interests of the others." (Philippians 2:3-4 – NIV)*

I understand this statement may be slightly confusing in light of the fact God has created all of us with equal worth. What Paul is insinuating is not that we would see ourselves as having less value, but that we have a choice to take the heart of a servant. In the process of serving another, we're valuing their need above our own in the moment.

I love how The Message puts it, *"Don't push your way to the front; don't sweet-talk your way to the top. Put yourself aside, and help others get ahead. Don't be obsessed with getting your own advantage. Forget yourselves long enough to lend a helping hand." (Philippians 2:3-4 – MSG)*

TO VALUE OTHERS ABOVE MYSELF

Understanding that many are in hot pursuit of whatever their selfish flesh desires, Paul is reaching into the deepest place within us to call us into alignment with our identity as followers of Christ. He's saying:

- Followers of Jesus don't live or work just for their own benefit.
- Followers of Jesus see tremendous value in everyone.
- Followers of Jesus lift others up rather than pushing them down.

These were revolutionary thoughts in Paul's day, and they are no less disruptive in our own. This way of life subverts the selfishness within all of us while infusing God's economy into any circumstance. To prefer someone over yourself is a way of expressing sacrificial love that follows in the footsteps of our Leader.

There is no better example of how to treat others than Jesus. He encountered the same types of people we come across every day – the rich, the poor, those who speak different languages, and those who have different belief systems. Jesus is our model, is He not?

The apostle Paul goes on to describe the humility of Jesus so beautifully:

"In your relationships with one another, have the same mindset as Christ Jesus: Who, being in very nature God, did not consider equality with God something to be used to his own advantage; rather, he made himself nothing by taking the very nature of a servant, being made in human likeness. And being found in appearance as a man, he humbled himself by becoming obedient to death - even death on a cross!" (Philippians 2:5-8 – NIV)

Paul starts with challenging us to "have the same mindset as Christ Jesus." He wants us to think about ourselves and the people around us in the same way that Jesus did. As I read the Scriptures, here's what I notice about Jesus:

- **Jesus didn't use his position for personal gain.**

  Jesus chose to step out of the spiritual realm of heaven into an earthly body to become a "servant" to all of humankind. He didn't come to hang out with the most popular in order to make a good name for Himself. Jesus came as God in the flesh to express His love for everyone – not just a certain group of people.

- **Jesus came to give – not to take.**

  He wasn't looking for people to laud Him as the next great ruler. He wasn't trying to rally a growing crowd of supporters to boost his ego. He wasn't seeking to take advantage of us. In contrast, Jesus came to bring hope and healing to the world. In Mark 10:44-45, Jesus says, *"Whoever wants to become great among you must be your servant, and whoever wants to be first must be slave of all. For even the Son of Man did not come to be served, but to serve, and to give his life as a ransom for many."* Jesus came to give.

- **Jesus was willing to sacrifice for others.**

  Jesus' idea of sacrifice wasn't giving up his "me time" to listen to the problems of a friend. The Scriptures tell us that He "humbled" himself and made the ultimate sacrifice for you and me – giving up His own life – to save us from our sins. This is the ultimate way that Jesus treated others better than Himself.

Are you challenged by these three lessons from the life of Jesus?

Think for a moment how can you use your position as a parent, neighbor, friend, or team member – not for your own gain – but for the benefit of others. In what relationship would you like to start "giving" more than you have in the past? Is there a sacrifice for the sake of another that God is nudging you to make?

The Example of My Mother

As I was growing up, I heard stories about my Mom's weekly adventures to the rural countryside surrounding Tenali. Joined by two or three other women, she would take a train or bus to a distant village that didn't have a Christian church.

Remember, these are the places to which Dalits have been banished, and no one else wants to go. The government hardly helps them, and their fellow Indians are convinced they are experiencing the karmic results of their past life. Higher castes believe they should just be left alone to deal with life on their own.

In contrast, my Mom took the Scriptures we've just studied very seriously. Not only did she take on the servant mindset of Christ, but she went out of her way to treat others better than herself – especially those who society sees as "less than" in some way.

She actually believed Jesus' commission for the 12 disciples is also for us today. He tells them, *"As you go, proclaim this message: 'The kingdom of heaven has come near.' Heal the sick, raise the dead, cleanse those who have leprosy, drive out demons. Freely you have received; freely give." (Matthew 10:7-8 – NIV)*

My Mom is greeted as she arrives.

After arriving at the edge of their destination, my Mom and her entourage of fellow servants would prayerfully approach what seemed to be a random home – almost always a single room with a mud floor and thatched roof.

Modestly dressed in beautiful saris, the women would be greeted by the poor Dalit family, who naturally welcomed them since nicely dressed visitors were completely unheard of. The family would be so happy that someone wanted to visit and talk with them.

If it sounds like the Dalits are oppressed and just thankful to have anyone paying any attention to them, you are correct. They have been abused and underprivileged to the point that any connection is welcomed. Not only was this true 30 years ago when my Mom began her ministry, but it's just as evident in modern-day India.

After sitting down, my Mom and her friends would be offered chai, and they would begin to ask questions about the household out of genuine interest and care.

"Tell me about your family."
"How many children do you have?"
"What are their names?"
"Do you have any needs in your life?"

Inevitably, they would end up at a family's home that had enormous challenges. Whether it was a severe illness, a couple's inability to get pregnant, or even demonic possession like you'd read about in the Bible, they never stumbled across a "healthy" household. It's like God gave them a divine radar to seek out those who were in desperate need of hope and healing.

After listening to all of the family's concerns, my Mom would share about the power of Jesus to transform their lives. She would describe Him as the One who came as God in the flesh to give us life to the full – an everlasting life.

"We would like to pray that Jesus would heal you. Is that okay?"

Because people in these desperate conditions fully recognize their deep need, they are willing to turn to Jesus as a possible Source. Having already tried pleading to Hindu gods, seeking the help of local shamans, and following superstitious practices, they're usually at the end of their rope with no where to turn.

Combine the desperation of the family with the faith of my Mom and her friends, and you've got a recipe for the miraculous. More often than not,

God seemed to do something inexplicable in the lives of that family, and the woman of the household would end up guiding my Mom by the hand to other neighbors in need.

The conversation would begin once again. Genuine questions for the family followed by my Mom sharing how Jesus had changed her life and ending with more prayer, hope, and healing. Before long, they were being fed and offered a place to stay for the night.

I'll never forget when I was 14 years old and on my first trip with my Mom to a rural village during summer break. Frustrated and disappointed, I would rather have been hanging out with friends than riding a bus for seven hours to Polavaram – not exactly a vacation destination by any means.

As we visited from house-to-house on the first day, we followed a local pastor to the home of a Dalit Hindu family. The husband and wife had been married for 10 years, but they still didn't have any children yet. As I've mentioned, this is not only a challenging experience for them as a couple, but there are cultural pressures at work as well.

With great faith, my Mom prayed for God's healing touch, and she strongly sensed He was going to give them children. After she shared about the love and power of Jesus, they chose to follow Him and were baptized the same day. My Mom challenged them to renounce all the Hindu gods they had been worshipping, and they agreed – even ridding their home of images and idols related to worship. As a symbol of their newfound faith and God's promise of a child, my Mom changed their names to Sarah and Abraham.

Within three months, my Mom received a letter in the mail from the woman...she was pregnant!

A year later, we went back to the same village, and there she was – waiting to greet us with a baby in her arms. What a huge party we had that day!

Just last year, I saw her once again, and she now has three grown children who are all married and followers of Jesus. What started on that initial trip to Polavaram with my Mom has resulted in an elderly home with 20 men and women, a children's home with 35 kids, and a church of over 100 people led by Pastor Blasamey. It's amazing to see what God has done there over the past 30 years.

I'm so thankful that my Mom embraced the mindset of Jesus and chose to value people that our culture sees as "less than." Through her sacrificial service, many lives have been touched for the glory of God.

Practical Ways to Value Others Above Ourselves
It is clear from the Scriptures that we all have equal value in the sight of God. Yet, we read the words of Paul calling us to "value others above yourselves, not looking to your own interests but each of you to the interests of the others."

It's interesting how we're prone to extremes when it comes to service.

Many of us are so concerned about a person taking advantage of us that we completely close ourselves off from the needs of others. On the other hand, some of us hide our co-dependence and 'need to please' under the guise of service and end up not meeting our own basic needs in the process.

No, you are not called to become everyone's doormat. No you can't fix everyone's problems. And, no, you are not Jesus. But, He is calling you to see tremendous value in every person – even "those" people. He is challenging you to lay aside your selfish interests and lift others up. Now, the question is, "How?"

1. **Move toward the need – not away from it.**

   In our most selfish moments, we close our eyes, turn our head, and walk away from the challenging issues (and people) around us. We act as if we don't see the problem, and we assume that someone else will take care of it. In our self-interest, we want to avoid being bothered with people who are different than us, people who are hurting, and people who are flat out inconvenient to deal with.

   One of the ways I have chosen to value others above myself is by setting aside my own comfort and moving toward a need rather than away from it.

   When I see the need, I choose not to retreat. I ask God for the strength to see the challenge for what it is and the wisdom to know what He's calling me to do in that very moment.

This was the case several years ago when my wife and I started recognizing the four-mile drive from our home to Harvest India's main ministry campus was limiting our influence among those who live and work there on a daily basis. With over 300 abandoned and orphaned children living in the dorms and 60 former prostitutes working in our Ashraya Project, we wondered if God was calling us to move our family onto the property.

Four miles away, the ministry bought a three-story home where my family and other leaders (25 plus people) have lived in Tenali for the past 15 years. In addition, teams from other countries stay in the guest rooms during their visits. Generous friends helped us add on and renovate over the years, and it had become an extremely comfortable living environment for our family. Frankly, we didn't want our children to continue growing up in a home that significantly varied in size or quality from the homes of those whom we serve.

Guest rooms for visiting teams - our previous home.

With this incredible opportunity to make a long-term investment in hundreds of lives coupled with the chance to downsize our living situation, we chose to build a new home on the Harvest India campus - a two-room cinder block house with a large patio for guests to come and visit. In the beginning, we constructed a thatched roof but over 100 rats quickly made their home in the multi-layered covering. It got so bad that we hung a large mosquito net over our bed to prevent rats from falling on top of us in the middle of the night. After one and a half years of enduring that mess, my wife finally put her foot down, and we installed a tile roof. Now that the rats are gone, it is our own piece of heaven, and we get to share it with a few hundred friends.

What would it look like for you to move toward a need rather than away from it? It may or may not involve a physical change of location. More likely, it's a movement of your heart – an infilling of compassion toward people in need and the courage to start taking action. You can do it. Start moving in that direction.

2. Be quick to lend a hand.

A few months back, one of our leaders hired a new staff member for his team, and the young man tagged along to welcome a group from the United States who was arriving on the train. When guests arrive, our staff is expected to grab their bags and carry them to the trucks standing by. This is a simple way we value others better than ourselves.

As the team was getting ready to jump in the cars, Gideon told the new staff member to pick up a bag, and the young man replied, "My job is to teach music to the kids…not to carry someone's bags."

The moment I heard his words, I jumped out of the car and picked up the bag myself to put it on top of the truck. I wanted him to know that no one – including me - is below picking up a bag and serving when there is a need. Let's just say he immediately ran over to grab the bag out of my hands…and he never said something like that again.

There are opportunities around us every day to quickly lend a hand. Whether it's holding open a door for someone whose arms are full, dropping off a bag of groceries to a single mom, or picking up the slack at work for someone who has fallen behind, you have the power to choose to prefer others above yourself.

Take a moment and compare the momentary inconvenience or cost to the magnitude of God's love that the other individual will experience through your tangible act of service.

Be ready. In the next 24 hours, you will have several occasions to lend a hand. Keep your eyes open. Look for ways to serve rather than be served.

3. **Leverage your position and power for the sake of others.**

   God has placed you in a position of influence and power. If you're a parent, you have a family and children. If you go to school, you have classmates. If you have a job, you are surrounded by colleagues. If you live in a neighborhood, you have neighbors.

   You may not have a prestigious title, but you have influence. Every single one of us has the ability to make an impact on the lives of others. The question is, "For what purpose are you leveraging your position and power?"

   When my Mom went from village to village, she was exerting influence for the benefit of others. She was a messenger of hope and healing to those who others looked down upon – people who were viewed as "less than."

   As you think about your sphere of influence – the place where God has you in this season of life, how can you leverage your position for the sake of those in need? Are there people who others ignore that you can begin to pay attention to? How can you serve the underserved in ways that truly benefit them?

   My guess is a person or group came to your mind immediately. You know who is struggling, and God has been tugging at your heart. It will require you to value them over your own comfort, but it will be worth it.

People May Not Understand, But Jesus Does

As you begin to make decisions that benefit others, some people around you may not understand. I'm not necessarily talking about those who you'll be serving. Sure, they may be surprised in the beginning, but their gratefulness will consume them soon after.

I'm talking about people who are close to you. Perhaps, your spouse, a parent, a co-worker, or a classmate. They'll start to ask questions like:

"Why would you do something like that?"

COMPELLED

"Don't you think that person should take care of themselves?"
"Aren't you afraid you're going to be taken advantage of?"

When my Mom made a decision to start ministering in rural villages, my grandfather said, "I think it would be better for you to die than for you to live this way. If you died, at least someone would have pity on your kids, and they would take care of them. Your life is a waste. Why did God give these children to you?"

My Mom would reply, "You don't know anything about my God. He is watching over us, and He will provide. He is everything in my life, and He will take care of them. You don't need to give me anything."

She was strong and consistent in her beliefs, and she saw God meet all of her needs – and ours as her children.

When my family started to build the cinder block home with a thatched roof, people in the US cried, "You could die from a roof fire started by people who don't like you. Or, cobras may come and attack you at night as they're hunting for rats."

Even my own brother asked, "What is wrong with you, Suresh? Do you have a screw loose?"

I just laughed - knowing that my God meets all my needs according to the riches of His glory. As a follower of Jesus, I'm choosing to live for the sake of others. I am setting aside my selfish desires and sacrificing my own comfort to lend a hand. I regularly embrace momentary inconvenience and treat it as a blessing from God. I am lifting others up so they may experience blessings in their own lives.

Who is God calling you to serve?

SMALL GROUP WEEK #5

Getting Started

1. In light of last week's discussion on increasing our dependence on God through prayer, what did you find yourself praying about over the past few days?

2. As we think about how we treat people in our world, which group of people do you the hardest time valuing, and why?

   a. People who look different than you.
   b. People who speak a different language.
   c. People who are less (or more) educated.
   d. People who live in a certain city or neighborhood.
   e. People who hold different beliefs.

3. Other than your parents, who has valued you in ways that touched your life? How did they show you that you were valuable?

Going Deeper

4. Read James 2:1-7. What stands out to you in this passage?

5. In your own words, how would you define favoritism? How is the act of favoring one over another connected to a person's value?

6. Read Philippians 2:3-8. How is Jesus an example of choosing to value the needs of others above our own?

7. As you read about Suresh's mother and the way she valued people who are often seen as "less than", who else came to mind? How have you witnessed that person value others above themselves?

Applying It To Your Life

8. Choose someone to re-read this paragraph: "It's interesting how we're prone to extremes when it comes to service. Many of us are so concerned about a person taking advantage of us that we completely close ourselves off from the needs of others. On the other hand, some of us hide our co-dependence and 'need to please' under the guise of service and end up not meeting our own basic needs in the process."

   Which "extreme" are you most prone to?

9. Suresh challenged us with three action steps at the end of this chapter.

   a. Move toward the need – not away from it.
   b. Be quick to lend a hand.
   c. Leverage your position and power for the sake of others.

   What would it practically look like to live out each one? (Discuss them one by one.)

10. Based on our conversation, is there someone God is bringing to mind? What would it practically look like to serve them (value them) this week?

CHAPTER 6

I AM COMPELLED BY A BURDEN FOR THE NEGLECTED

Each morning, I spend an hour connecting with people who come to my home in great need. Word of mouth has spread that Harvest India is a place of tangible help if you're hungry or hopeless, and there is usually a line of 10 to 20 people waiting.

We've talked with thousands of people who are seeking food, medical assistance, or even mediation over a conflict. Most of the conversations become a blur after so many years, but there are a few that have deeply touched me and changed the course of our ministry.

Around eight years ago, a man patiently waited in line to speak with me, and I couldn't help but stare over the shoulder of the person I was praying for.

With a filthy lungi pulled high around his thighs and an unbuttoned shirt hanging on his thin frame, he approaches me slowly, and a pungent odor soon follows. Out of respect, he raises his two fingerless hands in front of his disfigured nose as if he were going to pray.

"My name is Eswar, and I have traveled three hours to Tenali to ask for your help."

It is obvious this man has leprosy – missing fingers, deformed nose, and a skin condition that causes a blotchy whiteness on his normally dark skin.

"Sir, how can we help you?" I ask - assuming he wants money for food or perhaps to be seen by a doctor.

"I am living among 30 people who are starving in a leprosy camp many miles from this place. No one cares about us, and we don't know what to do. Can you help in some way?"

India has more cases of leprosy than any other nation.

While you may assume that leprosy is a long-forgotten disease you just read about in the Bible, it is still an issue in India – more than any other nation on the planet. In 2012 alone, 127,295 new cases of leprosy were diagnosed in my country. Leprosy is a contagious disease causing skin sores, nerve damage, and muscle weakness that worsens over time. Contrary to folklore, leprosy does not cause body parts to fall off, but they can become numb or diseased from secondary infections - resulting in tissue loss causing fingers and toes to become shortened and deformed, as cartilage is absorbed into the body.

While Dalits are generally avoided, lepers are physically ostracized from all aspects of Indian culture. In fact, there are numerous laws that make discrimination legal – including ordinances prohibiting lepers from obtaining a driver's license, traveling by train in some states, or running for election. Leprosy is even grounds for divorce in India!

People with leprosy are excommunicated from their community, and they live far away from their village in colonies with other lepers. Even if one member of your family contracts the disease, the entire family is forced to move away. Because no one will hire a leper, most spend the rest of their days walking into the nearest town to beg for food or money just to survive.

Despite the fact that physical touch is not a means of transmitting the disease, everyone avoids touching a leper at all cost.

Even though someone with leprosy may have money from begging, restaurants won't sell food to them, because it will inevitably hurt their business. Even to buy coffee at a roadside stand, a leper has to bring his or her own cup. And, if their state even allows them to ride the train, they have to sit in a designated area.

I think to myself, "How on earth can we help these people? Even the nation of India has turned its back on them in many ways...but Jesus doesn't."

As the man stands in the front of me waiting for a response, I am reminded of the words of Jesus: *"For I was hungry and you gave me something to eat, I was thirsty and you gave me something to drink, I was a stranger and you invited me in, I needed clothes and you clothed me, I was sick and you looked after me, I was in prison and you came to visit me." (Matthew 25:35-36 – NIV)*

Frankly, there is a tug of war going on inside me. As a small boy, I was taught that touching a leper would cause the disease to rub off on you, and my schoolmates and I always ran away from anyone with leprosy. On the other hand, I know this is Jesus standing in front of me - asking for help.

How can I *not* respond?

Looking him in the eye, I reach out to Eswar – taking his disfigured hands into mine – and say, “We will love you. Sit down and have some chai with me.”

I spent time hearing about the people he lives among and their plight to survive, and I promised him that we will do something to help. The very next month, we provided all 30 people with a large bag of rice, lentils, and some money – more help than they had ever been given.

As my staff and I reached out to embrace them and pray for them, they began to weep tears of joy, because no one had touched them in years. They hugged us over and over again – thankful for the simple gift of loving touch.

Eight years later, we now have over 600 people with leprosy who come to our campus every month to receive tangible support, prayer, and medical attention from Harvest India. To date, we have built 56 homes for over 200 people with leprosy in Boyapalam (1.5 hours from Tenali), and we are helping to build another colony in Bapatla.

Pursuing the Neglected

As we learned in the last chapter, Jesus calls us as His followers to recognize the inherent worth of every person and value others above ourselves - but I am challenged to take my service to a whole other level. Over the years, I have developed a strong burden for those who are outcast and discarded by society.

There is something inside of me that doesn’t want to just sit back and wait for opportunities to come my way. I could have easily prayed for Eswar, sent a load of rice out to the leper colony, and considered that my good deed for the day. Instead, I sensed God challenging me to pursue those who have been neglected.

This challenge originates from the heavy burden I carry in my heart. Once I hear about the intense needs of a group who has been neglected, I can’t get them out of my mind. I can’t stop thinking about their plight and processing how we could make a positive impact in some way. My heart feels the weight of their pain, and prayer doesn't make it go away.

Oftentimes, the burden just intensifies.

In Luke's account of Jesus' life, we read about a time when Jesus was invited to eat at the home of a prominent Pharisee. The guests for this meal seemed to think one's table position not only reflected one's status, but may actually create it. People were jockeying for position so that they could end up in seats of honor. Continuing the theme of valuing others above ourselves, Jesus tells them to take the lowest place.

"For all those who exalt themselves will be humbled, and those who humble themselves will be exalted." Then Jesus said to his host, "When you give a luncheon or dinner, do not invite your friends, your brothers or sisters, your relatives, or your rich neighbors; if you do, they may invite you back and so you will be repaid. But when you give a banquet, invite the poor, the crippled, the lame, the blind, and you will be blessed. Although they cannot repay you, you will be repaid at the resurrection of the righteous." (Luke 14:11-14 – NIV)

The host had no need to jockey for position, because his seat was already reserved. Yet, Jesus knew that the same spirit of selfishness was at work in both the guests and their host. Those who the host invites are those who can promote his social standing.

It's not just where one sits at the table that gives one status, but it's also who even gets invited to the meal. Jesus points out that when planning a dinner party, the temptation is to invite people who are most likely to help us in return. Remember, this is a parable. Don't get hung up on the example He uses. I realize you may not necessarily think of inviting wealthy people over for dinner because of something they can provide you in return.

Yet, we live in a culture where reciprocation is assumed.

If I do something for you, then I assume you'll do something for me – resulting in a somewhat fair exchange. I scratch your back – you scratch mine. This is learned early on among childhood friends, and it only gets more sophisticated as we grow up and carry out the practice in our families and in business. Jesus wants to turn reciprocation on its head.

Instead of hosting a dinner for people who can pay him back, the host is challenged by Jesus to pursue those who are neglected – people who could never return the favor.

The religious system of the Pharisees resulted in a divide between holy and unholy, the rich and the poor, the honored and the despised. If they actually pursued the neglected, the separation of those who were "better than" and those who were "less than" would disintegrate. Jesus' proposal would be the death of their whole way of life.

Since the neglected don't have a way to repay you, Jesus says, *"You will be repaid at the resurrection of the righteous."* In other words, if you are willing to value others above yourself and pursue the neglected, you will be giving evidence you have the kind of heart that is prepared to enter the Kingdom. This isn't a good deed that allows you to earn your way to heaven, but it is actual evidence you have chosen to follow in the footsteps of Jesus.

Jesus seems to be indicating the doors of His Kingdom are only open to men and women who humble themselves, and those who are bloated with arrogance and carrying the baggage of their own social status won't fit through the narrow door.

Who is Neglected in Your World?

Throughout the ministry of Jesus, he pursued people who no one else wanted to deal with. Although I'm well aware of who is neglected in India, I start to imagine who God might be calling you to pursue in the Western world. From my experience visiting the United States, Canada, and the United Kingdom, I'm wondering if these groups of people are neglected where you live:

- **Single Mothers**

  I have been amazed by the number of single moms I've met during my travels to the West, and I truly believe they are the equivalent to widows in my country. Although I hear there are many community services available to them, the absence of a father in the home (and oftentimes complete disappearance from the child's life) leaves the mother with the bulk (if not all) of the responsibility to raise their children.

  In India, widows are left in a similar condition – minus any social services. They often find backbreaking work in the nearby fields, and many end up giving their kids to relatives or even abandoning them at a children's home. The difficulty of earning a living, raising their children, and taking care of the basic needs of the household are beyond overwhelming – no matter if we're talking about a widow who lives in rural India or a single mother in the West.

James says, *"Religion that God our Father accepts as pure and faultless is this: to look after orphans and widows in their distress and to keep oneself from being polluted by the world." (James 1:27 – NIV)*

In other words, true religion – the real deal – isn't just about going to church every Sunday, checking off your daily quiet time, and tossing in a few bucks in the offering. It's about pursuing the neglected – orphans and widows in their distress.

The distress of a single mother can be the weight of earning her entire household's income or penny-pinching her welfare check. It's the challenge of helping get the homework done, tucking the kids into bed, and starting all over again - alone. And, in many cases, it can be the heartache of broken dreams and the anxiety of what the future may hold.

Do you know any single mothers who are in distress? Maybe you haven't pursued her enough to know the challenges she bears daily.

- **Foster Children**

With over 1,300 abandoned and orphaned children under our care, Harvest India is dedicated to embracing boys and girls who have somehow lost their families. While children's homes (ranging from 10 to 300 children) are common in India, I know that foster care is the predominant system implemented in the Western world.

I believe foster children – whether they live with a foster family or in a group home – are the modern-day orphans in your country. In most cases, their homes of origin are not safe situations for them to stay, and they may or may not ever return to living with their biological parents or relatives.

While the foster care system was created for the child to benefit from living in a stable home environment, I'm learning oftentimes that's far from the case. With children frequently moving from home to home (due to psychological and behavioral issues stemming from their homes of origin), the security needed to mature and develop is unavailable to them. On top of that, the sexual, physical, and psychological abuse many endure along the way is soul shattering.

What would happen if thousands of healthy, Christian families would begin to enroll as foster parents and do the hard work of providing these children (modern-day orphans) with a chance to grow up in a God-honoring home? What if our churches would develop ministries to support foster families? What if you found a creative way to invest in the life of a neglected child?

- **Immigrants**

Despite what your political persuasions may be, the Bible actually includes over 100 passages about welcoming, caring for, and loving the foreigner or stranger. Listen to the words of Moses to the people of Israel:

"For the LORD your God is God of gods and Lord of lords, the great God, mighty and awesome, who shows no partiality and accepts no bribes. He defends the cause of the fatherless and the widow, and loves the foreigner residing among you, giving them food and clothing. And you are to love those who are foreigners, for you yourselves were foreigners in Egypt." (Deuteronomy 10:17-19 – NIV)

He is reminding the Israelites of their time in exile – challenging them to remember what it was like to be a foreigner in a distant land. He called them to love the stranger and give them tangible help through food and clothing.

I realize that some of you are shouting "yes" while others are turning red in the face out of frustration or even anger. How one deals with the issue of immigration from a political perspective is quite tricky, but I can't disregard the fact that immigrants are some of the most neglected people in society. In fact, the law often gives us the right to live disconnected in our disdain, but Jesus calls us to be connected in love. God clearly calls us to care for them.

BY A BURDEN FOR THE NEGLECTED

Loving the foreigner or stranger was no less difficult in biblical times than it is today. It requires us to push through the fear of cultural and language differences and move to a place of radical inclusion. Not only does this mean embracing people who are different than us, but it also means that we don't try to change them. We love them as they are – trusting God to give us wisdom on how to truly be of benefit.

- **The Outcast**

I realize that "outcast" is a rather nebulous term, but my guess is it encompasses a wide variety of groups depending on where you live and what sphere of life you're in. Simply put, an outcast is someone who has been rejected by society or a particular social group.

In your school, who is the outcast? Is it the person who's just a bit awkward and doesn't quite fit in? Or, maybe it's the kid who wears all black and his skin is pale white? You are well aware of who gets pushed to the outside of social circles.

How about in your neighborhood? Is it the family who doesn't keep up their lawn or the people who speak a different language? Who is it? What about at work? Who is outcast there? The boss? The slacker? The guys who work in the warehouse?

Almost every sphere of life casts out the outsider, because they're different. Jesus calls us to pursue them. I've already shared about the Dalits and lepers in my country, but there's another group just as outcast. Thought to be a disease of the perverted or deviant, those with HIV and AIDS carry a heavy stigma in India, not unlike many other developing countries. Discrimination within the government, educational systems, and the culture at large runs rampant.

If someone contracts HIV, the person will go to any length to keep it a secret, because the societal repercussions are so great. If a parent has been infected, no one will ever want to marry his or her children. If a child has the disease, other parents won't want him or her to attend the local school. And, absolutely no one will ever want that person near the water well.

Every month we provide medicine to hundreds of patients with HIV.

Therefore, if a family finds out that a member of their household has the disease, the infected individual is often kicked out and ostracized – even a spouse. To cover up the loss, the household simply explains that the person died, and they never ever mention HIV or AIDS. By actually embracing the infected family member, the household takes a huge risk of being ostracized from their entire village.

Over 15 years ago, we started a ministry for those who were infected – providing medical care, food, and financial assistance. In fact, we've just opened our first AIDS hospice facility so that dying men and women can live out their final days surrounded by people who will love them and care for them.

I know what it's like to pursue people who are outcast. There's a risk of being misunderstood or even ostracized by your friends, family, or community. It's worth the risk, because this is the ministry Jesus has called us to. I trust that He will empower you to handle whatever He brings your way.

BY A BURDEN FOR THE NEGLECTED

The truth is there are people who are dying in this world – physically, emotionally, and spiritually – who have been neglected by their own community, and they need our tangible help. If we're waiting for them to appear on our doorsteps, we're going to miss out on the chance to be used by God in powerful ways. In His grace, God brought Eswar to my home that day, and I'm honored by the opportunity to pursue (and touch) the hundreds of lepers in our area.

Our Greatest Challenge – Feeling Overwhelmed

The biggest reason why we don't take action on behalf of the neglected is because it's overwhelming. I would be surprised if you were able to read through the description of the neglected in the last section (single mothers, foster children, immigrants, and the outcast) without feeling rather engulfed in the enormity of the need.

Feeling this way never motivates us to take action, and that's why I want to help us admit and overcome what we feel overwhelmed by:

1. **Are you overwhelmed by all the problems in our world?**

   Global hunger. Homelessness. Clean drinking water. Teen pregnancy. Human trafficking. Refugees of war. AIDS. Drug abuse. Urban violence. Overwhelmed yet? The sheer number of challenges can be depressing for anyone who has a desire to serve.

   The Antidote: *"Ask God to give you a burden for one issue."*

   If your heart hasn't been captured by a particular challenge, then go to God for direction. I bet something has already caught your attention though. What makes you angry? What gets your heart pumping? What causes your eyes to well up with emotion? What provokes you to start brainstorming solutions? Start there.

2. **Are you overwhelmed by the magnitude of the need?**

   The enormity of the problem may feel like a giant wave crashing on top of any hope you had to make a difference. The bottom line is that you and I can't fix the entire situation. It's just too big, too complex, and too consuming if we try to tackle it all at once.

The Antidote: *"Do for one what you wish you could do for everyone." (Andy Stanley)*

In order to move away from feeling overwhelmed by a problem, I want to invite you to embrace the words above from Andy Stanley (pastor of North Point Community Church in Atlanta, Georgia). You may be tempted to think, "If I can't fix the entire problem, why do anything at all?" This type of thinking is paralyzing. What if you started with one person?

That's what my Mom did. People may look at the breadth of Harvest India and marvel, but I remember when it was just my mother and her friends going from village to village. Instead of fixing the entire foster care system, what if you just invested in one child's life? What if your church came alongside the single mothers who are already part of the congregation? One person at a time.

3. Are you overwhelmed by possible discomfort or inconvenience?

This may step on a few toes, but I've never met more people who long for comfort and convenience than when I travel to the United States. So much of Western culture is centered on pursuing what's quick, easy, and pain-free. I know that serving and loving the neglected is not convenient at all, but doing something extraordinary isn't always going to be easy.

The Antidote: *"Embrace inconvenient blessings."*

In the process of serving, I have found that my discomfort is miniscule compared to what an individual has had to endure most of his or her life. Each time something is an inconvenience, I start looking for the blessing. Something about that moment is going to be a gift from God. Whether it's a hug from Eswar who has leprosy or the smile on the face of the woman after her cataract surgery, the amount of time and energy I spend with that person pales in comparison to the results. It's a blessing to them – and to me.

4. Are you overwhelmed by where to start?

Let's assume God has given you a burden for a particular issue or group of neglected people in the world. You realize you can only do your part, and you're up for a bit of discomfort or inconvenience in the process. Now, where do you start?

The Antidote: *"Partner with people who are already doing it."*

Rather than reinventing the wheel, look for an organization or group of people who have a similar burden. Don't believe you're an expert on the issue after reading a few articles online and watching a documentary. Be ready to learn, ask questions, and join in with what someone else is already doing. As you learn from them, God will guide you toward your next steps.

5. Are you overwhelmed by a lack of resources?

If the first thing you're worried about is raising a bunch of money to tackle an issue, think again. Most problems can begin to be addressed with a huge dose of creativity, passion, and love. When people start to see your heart for something, you'll be amazed how God starts to bring all sorts of resources your way.

The Antidote: *"Use what God has placed in your hand."*

In Exodus 4, God called Moses to go back to the place he had been running from and deliver the children of Israel out from under Pharaoh's heavy hand. Moses asks God what happens if the Israelites won't listen to him. God responds with a simple question, "What's in your hand?"

Moses had a simple staff in his hand, and God used it in a miraculous way (turning it into a snake) as a sign to the Israelites that God had truly appeared to him.

What has God already equipped you with? Maybe, you're talented in a certain way, and there's an organization that would benefit tremendously from your gifts. Perhaps, you're retired and have vast amounts of time on your hands. Or, maybe, God has blessed you with the ability to generate money, and He is calling you to leverage your financial resources.

I don't know what God has placed in your hands, but everyone has something to offer. You have resources – given to you by our Creator – that can bring hope and healing to the neglected who He has placed on your heart. Don't dismiss what you have to offer just because it's a natural gifting or comes easy to you. God can use everything!

Jesus Leads the Way
In the midst of our passion to help, let's not fall into the trap of setting ourselves up to be a hero. Jesus is the Hero. He is the one who is the ultimate example of serving those in need.

As news was starting to spread of His teachings and miracles, Jesus went to a synagogue in his hometown of Nazareth one day, was handed a scroll, and read from the prophet Isaiah: *"The Spirit of the Lord is on me, because he has anointed me to proclaim good news to the poor. He has sent me to proclaim freedom for the prisoners and recovery of sight for the blind, to set the oppressed free, to proclaim the year of the Lord's favor." (Luke 4:16-19 – NIV)*

This was the heart and soul of Jesus' ministry. He was (and is) focused on those who were neglected by society – those who were seen as "less than" in some way. Nothing has changed about the ministry of Jesus from then until now.

2,000 years later, Jesus is still proclaiming good news, unleashing freedom, healing the blind, and setting the oppressed free. The way He is doing it is through the power of the Holy Spirit at work through you and me.

Are you ready to join Him as He leads the way?

SMALL GROUP WEEK #6

Getting Started

1. We're all unique in some way. Go around the room and share two things that make you unique as a person.

2. As you read about Suresh's encounter with Eswar, the man with leprosy, were you surprised to hear that the disease still exists?

3. What do you think you would have done if you would have been in Suresh's shoes?

Going Deeper

4. Read Luke 14:1-14. Jesus seems to point out both the behavior of the guests and the behavior of the host. What is Jesus concerned about?

5. How does Jesus demonstrate in His own life what He's calling the guests and host to?

6. Suresh highlighted several groups of neglected people in the West – single mothers, foster children, immigrants, and the outcast. Who else do you see that's neglected in our culture?

Applying It To Your Life

7. As you think about neglected people in our culture, do you find yourself motivated to help, overwhelmed, indifferent, or something else?

8. If you're overwhelmed (like many people), do you find that you're weighted down by…

a. All the problems of the world?
b. The magnitude of the need?
c. Possible discomfort or inconvenience?
d. Where to start?
e. Lack of resources?

9. Read Luke 4:16-19. How are you sensing that Jesus is leading you to follow in His footsteps? What practical next steps are you feeling called to?

CHAPTER 7

I AM COMPELLED TO BELIEVE NOTHING IS IMPOSSIBLE WITH GOD

Each year, at least a dozen teams from other countries come to India to see the work of the ministry, and our staff of over 100 people invests many hours preparing their itinerary and ensuring all the details of their experience are set. When they arrive in India, we make sure they get a chance to visit:

- The main Harvest India campus housing over 300 abandoned and orphaned children.
- The new Harvest India school with over 500 children in attendance.
- Our Tenali medical clinic where we see numerous patients free of charge each week.
- One of our nursing schools where we educate Dalit girls to be employed by local hospitals.
- A water well dedication in a rural village that's getting clean drinking water for the first time.
- A vibrant church service where they share a message of encouragement.
- And many more places where God is at work!

During every trip, something profound takes place – both in the lives of the team and through the hands-on ministry they carry out. The opportunities in India are endless. Everywhere you turn, you can see God doing what many consider to be impossible.

I'm reminded of one such experience 10 years ago when a team from the United States was visiting. Our staff was planning to take them four hours away to Peddapuram for a series of nighttime outreach meetings and daytime house-to-house ministry.

For weeks, my leaders partnered with the local Harvest India pastor to find a suitable meeting venue, usually a large field near an event center or public building. In advance of the team's arrival, we have people distribute flyers and hang posters in the area to announce the services. We even hire a rick-shaw driver to take one of our team members throughout area villages to announce the service times and location over a loudspeaker. As the stage and sound system are set up, word starts to spread that something exciting is happening in town. Because Americans are coming, there is great interest in showing up to see these "white people" – even though many on the team come from a variety of ethnic groups.

We pray for people to be healed everywhere we go.

On the morning of the first outreach meeting, we take the visiting team to a nearby village to visit from house to house and pray with people. As the team begins to wander around the dirt roads, we get word that the local Hindu priest's wife - Thulasi - is very sick with stomach cancer.

TO BELIEVE NOTHING IS IMPOSSIBLE WITH GOD

As my Mom and I walk into the couple's home with a few members of the visiting team, we all immediately realize the woman is in bad shape. Surrounded by Hindu idols they've worshipped for a lifetime, the woman is lying on a cot with her stomach bulging from the growth of the tumors - looking as if she is seven months pregnant.

"Good morning, Thulasi. Can we pray for you?"

Silence. Nothing can be heard except for the crying of her family gathered around. She can't even open her eyes, and she's not moving at all. Doctors have given her days to live.

As the team gathers around and prays passionately for her, Thulasi's family weeps loudly over her impending death. There is a sense of human helplessness in moments like these. The doctors can do nothing. Her husband – a Hindu priest – has placed offerings at the temple day after day, and he has called out to many gods to no avail.

We realize there's nothing we can do at this point other than pray and have faith that God can do the impossible. After laying hands on the woman, we're all wiping tears from our eyes as we step out of the couple's home. For some, this is the first time they've ever experienced something so dark and hopeless.

"How did things even get to this point?"
"Isn't there something the doctors can do?"
"I can't believe we're just going to leave the woman this way."

After seeing thousands upon thousands of Indians struggle with poverty and disease, I've stopped asking these questions. Stepping into that darkness is just too much for me to bear. It's a cyclone of never-ending questions fueled by hopelessness and despair.

Instead, I have learned to focus on my only hope. Jesus.
I know it may sound trite, but I don't have anywhere else to turn.

When a couple can't seem to get pregnant…
When a child inexplicably dies…
When a ferry collapses and a dozen people drown…
When a tsunami hits the coast of India like it did in 2004…

The only thing I can do is put my hope and faith in the One works miracles. Why? Because I've seen God do the "impossible" time after time.

The next morning, as the team is sitting down for breakfast in a neighboring village, a young man arrives – out of breath and full of excitement. It was Thulasi's son-in-law with some "impossible" news.

Thulasi was healed!

In the middle of the night, she saw a man dressed in all white come into her room, and he reached out to touch her stomach. Then, with enough strength to get out of bed, she found her way to the bathroom, and she felt the tumor pass out of her body and into the toilet. When the rest of the family woke up, she had already taken a shower, and she was sweeping the house.

Her daughter, a high-profile doctor from Kakinada, had come to visit and say good-bye, but now she was celebrating this "impossible" medical miracle. Not only did their family leave the Hindu temple, but they threw away all their idols and became followers of Jesus.
Nothing is impossible with God. Those words were spoken by Gabriel – an angel sent to deliver some "impossible" news to a young teenage girl.

"Gabriel appeared to her and said, "Greetings, favored woman! The Lord is with you!" Confused and disturbed, Mary tried to think what the angel could mean. "Don't be afraid, Mary," the angel told her, "for you have found favor with God! You will conceive and give birth to a son, and you will name him Jesus. He will be very great and will be called the Son of the Most High." (Luke 1:28-32 – NLT)

This young girl – probably around 13 years of age – had to be completely confused by this encounter. Number one – she's talking to an angel. Number two – this angel is telling her that she's going to have a baby before she marries the young man she's engaged to. Let's just say that's a slight problem in her day.

"Mary asked the angel, "But how can this happen? I am a virgin." The angel replied, "The Holy Spirit will come upon you, and the power of the Most High will overshadow you. So the baby to be born will be holy, and he will be called the Son of God. What's more, your relative Elizabeth has become pregnant in her old age! People used to say she was barren, but she has con-

ceived a son and is now in her sixth month. For nothing is impossible with God." (Luke 1:34-37 – NLT)

If you've been a Christian for quite some time, it can be easy to miss how ludicrous all this sounds. A virgin is going to give birth to a baby, and her old relative is going to have a child, too! The angel knows how crazy this sounds, and he reassures her with powerful words in the midst of this great mystery.

For nothing is impossible with God.

That's not only true in the case of Mary - the eventual mother of Jesus, but it's true for you and me. We have the opportunity to respond with faith as soon as we encounter a mystery.

"Mary responded, "I am the Lord's servant. May everything you have said about me come true." (Luke 1:38 – NLT)

In the midst of a mysterious and challenging situation, she chooses to put her faith in God – trusting that God has a plan for her life. I wonder what would happen if we developed a genuine reaction like hers when things don't seem to add up in the natural realm.

Faith Is Not a Feeling

We tell people, "Put your faith in Jesus Christ, and He will forgive all your sins." And, yes, He does. This often-emotional experience is a transformative time for the new Christian, but that feeling is soon to wane in the days, weeks, or months as challenges come our way. It can be tempting to believe that a certain emotional experience is evidence of "having faith".

Yet, faith is not a feeling we experience.
It's a choice to trust in the midst of the mysterious.

Faith isn't just something you "have" – it's something you "do". Faith is a verb! *Faithing* is the act of believing that all things are possible with God. Rather than waiting for a feeling to come upon you, you can actually faith that God is going to do something miraculous in the midst of your mysterious situation.

So many things in life are a mystery, aren't they? Anytime something painful or challenging or confusing happens in my life, I know it can be tempting to go down the road of asking, "Why? Why? Why?" Although many in the Scriptures asked this question as well, it might just have to remain a mystery on this side of eternity.

In those moments, I am learning to choose to *faith* – putting my hope in the One who holds the whole world – and my life – in the palm of His hand. God is not far off in the distance wondering when I'm going to catch up. No, he is walking with me in the midst of the mystery. I trust that He has a plan, and I find peace in knowing He'll never leave me.

The Bible says, *"And without faith it is impossible to please God, because anyone who comes to him must believe that he exists and that he rewards those who earnestly seek him." (Hebrews 11:6 – NIV)*

That's a strong statement, isn't it? The Bible is saying we can't please God without *faithing*. It says we must believe He exists and that He rewards those who seek Him. This "belief" in God goes far beyond a mental assent He exists as some cosmic being. The belief the Bible is talking about is a deep-down understanding that God is all-powerful, all-knowing, and always present. It's a trust that He is the One to turn to no matter what is happening in our lives, and the result is that we will be rewarded in some way.

I remember the first time I mailed a package to the United States, and I was so concerned about how it was going to get there. After questioning the man behind the counter for several minutes, I finally trusted that the box would arrive at its final destination.

Can you imagine if I would not have put my faith in the shipping company? Envision me sitting next to the package waiting for the driver to pick it up. Picture me questioning the driver about his care for the package, the next stop, and who would handle it next.

He would have probably ended up saying, "Hey buddy, why don't you just deliver the package yourself?"

The truth is I would rather have taken it there myself, but I didn't have the time or money to get there and back. In other words, it was impossible for me to get the package to its destination without *faithing* that the shipping company would be able to deliver it.

Even though I didn't know exactly how they were going to get it there (a mystery), I trusted that they had the resources needed in order to pull it off. The same thing is true about God. Just because the process (and even the final outcome) are unknown to us doesn't mean that it's a mystery to Him. He is simply asking us to put our faith in Him – to *faith* that He can do the impossible.

Three Reasons Why God Can Do the Impossible

In the midst of life's challenges, I have to remind myself of the basic truths of our faith. While I would love a specific word of divine wisdom tailored for my exact situation, it's just as powerful to re-focus on the character of who God is.

- **God is everywhere.**

  The Bible teaches us that God is present in every space with His whole being. The heavens cannot contain Him, and He is always nearby. He is everywhere – all the time.

  "Where can I go from your Spirit? Where can I flee from your presence? If I go up to the heavens, you are there; if I make my bed in the depths, you are there. If I rise on the wings of the dawn, if I settle on the far side of the sea, even there your hand will guide me, your right hand will hold me fast." (Psalm 139:7-10 - NIV)

  While some of us have defaulted to an image of God as being a old grandfather seated off in the distant heavens, nothing could be further from the truth. We see from the encounters of our forefathers that God is close to us, and He is not limited by time or space as we know it.

  God can be keenly aware of the details of your life – empowering you to get through your circumstances – while He's simultaneously speaking words of life into me halfway around the globe. God has an unlimited ability to be present, because He is already present everywhere.

- **God knows everything.**

  God is not limited in His knowledge. He knows every decision, action, motivation, or possibility from the beginning of time and throughout eternity. He doesn't know about one thing more than another, because He knows things immediately, simultaneously, comprehensively, and truly.

Can you even fathom that?

"Who has understood the mind of the LORD, or instructed him as his counselor? Whom did the LORD consult to enlighten him, and who taught him the right way? Who was it that taught him knowledge or showed him the path of understanding?" (Isaiah 40:13-14 - NIV)

In other words, God has never learned anything.
He has always known everything.

"O LORD, you have searched me and you know me. You know when I sit and when I rise; you perceive my thoughts from afar. You discern my going out and my lying down; you are familiar with all my ways. Before a word is on my tongue you know it completely, O LORD." (Psalm 139:1-4 - NIV)

If you believe that God hates you and He's out to catch you doing something wrong, then the fact that God knows everything probably fuels your fear. Yet, if you understand that God is love and His knowledge of your life is a source of security, then you will join me in resting deeply in the reality that God cares for each one of us intimately.

- **God is all-powerful.**

We see from the Scriptures (both in word and deed) that God has the power to do anything He chooses, but He also has the ability to withhold His power according to His will.

"Ah, Sovereign Lord, you have made the heavens and the earth by your great power and outstretched arm. Nothing is too hard for you." (Jeremiah 32:17 – NIV)

No, there is not. God created the heavens and the earth, and He begins and ends life daily. He transforms the heart of a sinner and redeems the brokenness of individual lives. Nothing is more or less difficult for God.

"I am the LORD, the God of all mankind. Is anything too hard for me?" (Jeremiah 32:27 – NIV)

TO BELIEVE NOTHING IS IMPOSSIBLE WITH GOD

> Your health problem, your broken marriage, or your prodigal child – none of them are too hard for God. Even the hardest heart that's entirely self-sufficient is not too difficult for God to touch. After telling his disciples how challenging it is for a rich man to enter the Kingdom of God, they ask Him, "Who then can be saved?"
>
> *"Jesus looked at them and said, "With man this is impossible, but with God all things are possible." (Matthew 19:26 – NIV)*
>
> God has the power to redeem the life of someone who is consumed by anything – money, drugs, pride, or even religiosity.

Because God is always present, all-knowing, and all-powerful, I have chosen to believe that "nothing is impossible with God." God is all around us, and He knows exactly what's going on in our world and in our individual lives. He is not blind or deaf or distracted. He knows everything, sees everything, and has the power to do anything.

People ask me all the time why miraculous signs and wonders don't happen that often in the Western world, and they don't seem to like my answer:

- You listen to miraculous stories on Sunday, but you don't really believe.
- You have your own plan and agenda that leaves very little room for God.
- You don't need to depend on God, because you already have Plan A, Plan B, and Plan C all figured out.
- When you do turn to God, it's because Plans A through C didn't work out.

In India, with such great poverty and limited access to resources that the West often takes for granted, we only have prayer in most cases. Rather than seeing prayer as something we do when all other options have been exhausted, we consider *faithing* in God our first step.

I believe we're experiencing God's miraculous power at work among us, because we believe in Him – not just an intellectual belief – but a "I don't have another option" belief. He is everything to us, and we have nothing else that even compares to Him.

Instead of thinking these experiences were just for the disciples, what if you started to actually believe God could do the "impossible" in your life?

The Psalmist tells us to *"taste and see that the Lord is good." (Psalm 34:8 – NIV)* You have seen God's miraculous goodness at work in places like India, but you may not have tasted it.

You have read about Peter and John going up to the temple to pray when they came across a man who couldn't walk. Peter says, *"Silver or gold I do not have, but what I do have I give you. In the name of Jesus Christ of Nazareth, walk." Taking him by the right hand, he helped him up, and instantly the man's feet and ankles became strong." (Acts 3:6-7 – NIV)*

Have you been walking by the "impossible" without stretching out your hand? The Bible is telling us that we must believe in God – confident in the fact that He is always present, always knowing, and always powerful. We serve a big God who wants to do big things in you - and through you.

The brother of Jesus writes, *"Do not merely listen to the word, and so deceive yourselves. Do what it says." (James 1:22 – NIV)* This doesn't mean that we're just supposed to act Christian by being nice to everyone. It also means that we're called to do the things Jesus did.

In fact, Jesus says, *"Very truly I tell you, whoever believes in me will do the works I have been doing, and they will do even greater things than these." (John 14:12 – NIV)*

Greater things? That's what He said. I'm challenging you to quit living to satisfy yourself. Don't just show up at church every week and think that's what it means to follow Jesus. May you be compelled to believe that nothing is impossible with God!

Where Can God Do the Impossible?
After teaching a crowd of people, Jesus got into a boat and his disciples followed after Him. While they set sail across the lake, Jesus decided to take an untimely nap. A furious storm arose, and water was sloshing over the sides.

"The disciples went and woke him, saying, "Lord, save us! We're going to drown!" He replied, "You of little faith, why are you so afraid?" Then he got up and rebuked the winds and the waves, and it was completely calm. The men were amazed and asked, "What kind of man is this? Even the winds and the waves obey him!" (Matthew 8:25-27 – NIV)

TO BELIEVE NOTHING IS IMPOSSIBLE WITH GOD

This is one of few times we see in the Bible when Jesus performed a miracle when there was a lack of faith around Him. In almost every other case, someone's faith was a catalyst for Jesus to do the "impossible" in someone's life. This was a defining moment for the disciples – an opportunity for Jesus to emphasis the importance of faith in Him.

You may remember another occasion in the Bible when a man kneels before Jesus and begs him to help his son who has seizures, because the disciples could not heal him.

"Bring the boy here to me." Jesus rebuked the demon, and it came out of the boy, and he was healed at that moment. Then the disciples came to Jesus in private and asked, "Why couldn't we drive it out?" He replied, "Because you have so little faith. Truly I tell you, if you have faith as small as a mustard seed, you can say to this mountain, 'Move from here to there,' and it will move. Nothing will be impossible for you." (Matthew 17:17-20 – NIV)

Not only is nothing impossible for God, but Jesus is telling us that nothing is impossible for us if we have faith as small as a mustard seed. This faith is built upon an understanding that God exists everywhere, knows everything, and has the power to do anything.

1. **God can heal your mind and body.**

   Many of us are challenged physically, and God is constantly healing us. Think about the last cold you caught – God healed you. Remember when you got a cut and it scabbed over – that was God healing you. All those times you went to the doctor and took medicine – God was healing you.

   You're already quite experienced with healing, but I believe God wants to use you to miraculously heal yourself and others in ways that you may think are "impossible".

   Seven years ago in the Bandalagaruvu children's home, there was an 8-year-old orphaned child named Rambabu playing in a nearby field with other boys. As he was running for a ball, a black snake jumped out and bit his ankle. Both Rambabu and a friend confirmed it was indeed a venomous cobra as they saw it slither away.

In that rural area, there are no hospitals or first aid centers, and it's two hours to the nearest medical facility. Within 30 minutes, the little boy's body was turning blue and rigid, and phlegm was coming out of his mouth.

All 40 of the children in the home started to pray – with faith – that God would do the "impossible" and save their friend. After 30 minutes of passionate intercession, Rambabu slowly awakened out of his venom-induced coma with the entire village surrounding him. By the time a doctor and I reached the home, the boy was standing on his own two feet.

There was nothing for us to do other than marvel at the two fang marks on his ankle. He was completely healed that day, and he's now 15 years old and enrolled in college.

Why doesn't God heal like this every time? It's truly a mystery. Even though I don't have a complete understanding of God's ways, He never called me to be the one who does the healing. God just calls me to pray. That's why I keep doing my part and trust Him with the results.

2. God can multiply your finances.

Several years ago, Harvest India had very little money to spend on Christmas. Although the basic needs of our ministry were covered (barely), we didn't have the finances to buy all our orphan children, staff, and teachers (almost 2,000 people) the gift of a new outfit – the only special present they receive all year. We were also planning to cancel our Christmas Eve dinner where we usually feed over 2,000 needy people in Tenali as a way to bless them in Jesus' name.

We would need close to $25,000 to cover the gifts and dinner. I was disappointed to say the least, but I sensed God was asking me to put my faith in His ability to do the impossible.

In faith, I authorized my staff to place the order on December 1st with our clothing supplier – knowing that we would be able to pay the invoice before the arrival of the gifts. With each passing day, I cried out to God for miraculous provision. By December 20th, there was still no money to pay for the presents. My entire family and staff were praying and fasting for God to provide the money, and on December 22nd, one generous person made a donation for $25,000 that paid for everything. God provides exactly what we need and right on time. A true Christmas miracle!

You and I both know that money can be one of the greatest sources of stress in our lives. It can be overwhelming to earn, spend, save, and invest. The greatest challenge for many is the discipline to only spend what is earned. While I wouldn't necessarily recommend that you spend $25,000 without having the money in hand, I do know I needed to be obedient to God's direction in that moment.

Yes, Deuteronomy 6:16 says, *"Do not put the Lord your God to the test,"* but I'm not testing to see if God is real or faithful. I'm being obedient to what I sense God is calling me to do.

There's no excuse for reckless spending and mismanagement. It seems odd to ask God to miraculously rescue us from our own misdeeds. Wouldn't it be wiser to honor God with our finances, ask for His grace in the areas where we've messed up, and have faith that He'll multiple what we already have?

Solomon writes, *"Honor the Lord with your wealth, with the firstfruits of all your crops; then your barns will be filled to overflowing, and your vats will brim over with new wine." (Proverbs 3:9-10 – NIV)*

I want God to be honored by the way that I handle money. By giving back to Him, I'm telling Him – and reminding myself – that He is the source of everything I have been blessed with. I want you to know that I'm praying and *faithing* that God can do a miracle in your finances as well.

3. God can restore your broken relationships.

With a divorce rate of 40-50% in the West, broken relationships are something that we encounter on a daily basis. Whether it's a husband and wife who can't get along or children who distance themselves from their parents or two friends who have allowed a misunderstanding to come between them, relational fractures are some of the most painful experiences in our lives. While most of this brokenness is the result of selfishness, pride, poor communication, and a lack of forgiveness (on both sides), God can do a miraculous work in your heart. Since you can't control the other person, the only thing you can work on is your own thoughts, attitude, and behavior. What got you into the mess isn't going to get you out of it.

"Trust in the Lord with all your heart and lean not on your own understanding; in all your ways submit to him, and he will make your paths straight." (Proverbs 3:5-6 – NIV)

We often turn to this passage when we're faced with a difficult decision, but what if we stopped leaning on our present understanding of how to deal with the broken relationship? Obviously, that approach hasn't worked up until this point in time.

I know that God can work a miracle in your heart and in any relationship where there has been hurt or disconnection. Do you have faith that God can do something? (Remember, faith isn't a feeling – it's a verb.)

4. God can expand your influence.

From the moment we purchased the 20-acre Harvest India campus, my Mom wanted to construct a church building, but the needs of other ministries always seem to take precedent.

Breaking ground on the main children's home on our 20-acre campus.

One by one, we built the main children's home, a Bible college, and then the Ashraya Project facility. She passed away without ever seeing that part of her vision come to fruition, but it lived on in the hearts of our team.

Several years ago, a college started construction on a new campus that would accommodate over 15,000 college students directly adjacent to our facility. In that moment, God was very clear with His message to our team, "It's time to build the church."

I immediately called Venu, an architectural engineer who handles all our building needs, to get to work on the plans. As I shared my dream for a three-story church in the shape of a cross with a ground floor community center, he started laughing and said, "This guy is always thinking crazy stuff. This will be the biggest building in the area!"

Without any money to invest on the project, I heard God say, "Put a cornerstone in the ground and pray."

We poured a two feet by two feet block of solid concrete, attached a dedication plaque, and invited a visiting team from the US to pray for God to do the "impossible".

Because of God's miraculous provision through generous donors, I'm happy to report we're almost done building a church that will seat 3,000 people, and we know that God will bring His work to completion as we are *faithing* for the resources to purchase the plumbing, electrical, painting, and furniture.

When we bought the 20-acre campus, we had no idea that a college was going to build on the property next to ours. When God put the vision of a church into my Mom's heart, she had no clue God was preparing to extend our influence by bringing 15,000 English-speaking young people to us. We had no idea, but God did. He had a plan to do the "impossible" all along.

My guess is there's something in your life that seems "impossible" in this very moment. Whether it's in your family, your finances, your health, or your personal dreams, you may be having a hard time believing God actually wants to do something.

COMPELLED

When things aren't adding up and you don't know what to do, there is only One who is able to come through. Will you trust Him that His timing is perfect?

Remember, faith is not a feeling we experience.
It's a choice to trust in the midst of the mysterious.

Knowing that God is always present, all-knowing, and all-powerful, will you join me in *faithing* that He can do the impossible in our lives?

SMALL GROUP WEEK #7

Getting Started

1. If nothing was impossible, what would you want to do or experience in life?

2. Have you ever had the chance to visit Harvest India? If so, what was the experience like?

Going Deeper

3. Hebrews 11:6 says, *"And without faith it is impossible to please God, because anyone who comes to him must believe that he exists and that he rewards those who earnestly seek him."* If you starting to think of "faith" as a verb (something you do – i.e., faithing) not just as a noun (something you have), how do you think that would impact your life?

4. Suresh points out three reasons why God can do the impossible.

   a. God is everywhere.
   b. God knows everything.
   c. God is all-powerful.

   As you think about the events of the Bible, where can you see these statements to be true?

5. Read Matthew 17:17-20. Do you really believe this? Why or why not?

Applying It To Your Life

6. Although there are many "impossibilities" that God can overcome, four specific examples were highlighted:

   a. God can heal your mind and body.
   b. God can multiply your finances.
   c. God can restore your broken relationships.
   d. God can expand your influence.

   Which one of these four is easiest for you to believe? Which one is the hardest?

7. As you think about your current season of life, what seems impossible for you to overcome, and why?

8. Suresh writes, "Faith is not a feeling we experience. It's a choice to trust in the midst of the mysterious." What does this statement mean to you?

9. Take time to break into smaller groups of two to three people. Pray for God to give each other faith to trust Him in the midst of the mysterious.

CHAPTER 8

I AM COMPELLED TO PRESS ON IN THE FACE OF ADVERSITY

With the wide variety of people, places, and cuisine in our country, one could easily call India a nation of *diversity*, but a more apt description is a nation of *adversity*. While I love my homeland, I am a bit jealous of the organization and consistency that can be found in Western countries. On any given day…

- Power may go out mid-day as electricity is diverted to large businesses.
- Rain pours down at a moment's notice.
- Roads flood and traffic is diverted.
- Church services start late as the pastor waits for people to come in from the harvest fields.
- A Hindu burial processional may cause traffic to come to a standstill.
- A political protest may cause a town to become unsafe.

Even as I write these words, there are people within our state (Andhra Pradesh) that want to divide the government and land in half. Their way of going about this involves physically blocking roads by living in the middle of them. Can you imagine if protesters set up tents in the middle of your main streets and starting sleeping, eating, and washing themselves?

It's pure madness!

No matter how much our staff plans, there are so many things out of our control. Visiting teams from the West find the chaotic atmosphere a bit amusing and often rather frustrating.

They quickly learn that adversity is an opportunity for perseverance.

In 2004, we planned to take a visiting team from the United States to Narsipatnam, an area where Hindus have strong ties to the Communist political party and usually don't believe in God. With no strong Christian churches in the area, we decided to hold a three-day crusade because of the great need.

After securing the open field to host the event, we immediately encountered strong opposition from local Communist leaders. As we began to put up wall posters through the city, people came along behind us and tore them down. Word was spreading quickly about our plans, and it was not being received as "good news."

In the face of opposition, we chose to persevere – knowing that God had called us to be a blessing to the people in this place.

As our staff was setting up for the event, 20 people jumped out of their vehicles and came running toward them with cricket bats and iron rods. These angry men tore down our tents, broke apart the stage, bashed in the speakers, and ripped down the screens. Not only did they destroy our equipment, but they turned their wrath on our staff – severing beating seven of them and breaking the leg of another.

"We will kill you if you come again," they yelled as they jumped back into their vehicles and sped away.

Not only were our staff members disheartened from taking a physical beating, but we found out the equipment rental company didn't have insurance and we were going to have to pay for it all.

As I gathered our team together, I reminded them of the words of the Apostle Paul who faced more adversity than any of us put together: *"Forgetting what is behind and straining toward what is ahead, I press on toward the goal to win the prize for which God has called me heavenward in Christ Jesus." (Philippians 3:13-14 – NIV)*

I told them to think about why we chose this difficult place, "There are people living in Narsipatnam who don't know Jesus, and they are living in darkness. We're pressing on! God sent us here to do the work. If we want to have freedom, we have to fight for freedom. If we sit back, no one will have freedom in their lives. We must work hard to present the freedom of Christ to these people."

I immediately contacted my powerful friend who is a government official in Hyderabad, and he put a call in to the local police department. Within a few hours, the Narsipatnam chief of police was knocking on the door of my hotel room, and he assured me everything would go well from that point forward.

God had something incredible planned, but I didn't know it was going to be this big. On the first night of the crusade, over 5,000 people showed up, and God miraculously healed many men and women. After 10,000 people attended on the second night, a huge crowd of over 20,000 packed the giant field on the final evening of the crusade.

Lives are being changed through the power of God's love.

As I stood on the reconstructed stage, I looked out over the sea of faces and thanked God for His strength that allowed us to persevere in the face of adversity. We could have canceled the event in the name of safety. We could have postponed the crusade for another time. We could have said "no" to God's call on our lives. Instead, we persevered.

The result - over 8,000 people chose to follow Jesus during those three nights, and we have established 10 strong churches in the area since that time.

How NOT to Respond to Adversity
When a challenge comes our way in life, I find that many people respond in one of two ways that are less than compelling:

- **Aggression**

  How easy it would have been for us to pick up metal rods and go looking for the men who beat our staff members! You better believe I was angry, but I know that aggression only escalates the problem. More bad decisions are made in the midst of anger than any other time. Our view of the situation is often distorted, and our ability to hear God's voice is diminished.

  "Make sure that nobody pays back wrong for wrong, but always strive to do what is good for each other and for everyone else. Rejoice always, pray continually, give thanks in all circumstances; for this is God's will for you in Christ Jesus." (1 Thessalonians 5:15-18 – NIV)

  Paying back wrong for wrong only causes the environment to become more heated, and we won't move toward the ultimate results we truly desire. If you're prone to anger and aggression when things don't go your way, may I suggest developing the discipline of celebrating, praying, and giving thanks? That's what the Apostle Paul is suggesting in the Scriptures above.

  As you hear the challenging news, what would happen if you started to find things to rejoice or celebrate about? "God, I want to celebrate the fact that my staff members are alive and will fully recover."

  What would it be like if you started to pray as soon as adversity came your way? "God, I ask you to touch the hearts of the men who attacked us. Protect us from anything else going wrong and give us wisdom about our next steps."

How would your attitude change if you began to look for a solution with thankfulness in your heart? "God, thank you for the opportunity to be here in Narsipatnam. Thank you for providing for all our needs. You are a good God!"

It's easy to allow aggression to carry us down a hasty path, but it's not an emotion I want to be compelled by.

- **Apprehension**

If you're not prone to aggression, my guess is you're inclined to be apprehensive in the face of adversity. Apprehension is an anxiety or fear that something bad is going to happen – usually based on our previous experiences.

If we allowed fear (or apprehension) to consume us after the men came and destroyed the stage, we would have missed out on something amazing God had planned for the people of Narsipatnam.

David writes, *"The Lord is my light and my salvation - whom shall I fear? The Lord is the stronghold of my life - of whom shall I be afraid?" (Psalm 27:1 – NIV)*

In no way am I suggesting that we be reckless in our actions and not take every aspect of a situation into account. We should use godly wisdom as we approach adversity, but fear will distract us from courageously saying "yes" to what God wants to do in us and through us.

You'll notice I used wisdom to contact government authorities, and God gave us favor with the local law enforcement. If I had been consumed with apprehension, I wouldn't have had the courage to even make that call.

In moments like these, I'm inspired by the words of Moses to Joshua as he stood on the edge of the Promised Land: *"Be strong and courageous. Do not be afraid or terrified because of them, for the LORD your God goes with you; he will never leave you nor forsake you." (Deuteronomy 31:6 – NIV)*

Our strength and courage is rooted in the fact that God is with us, and He'll never leave us nor forsake us. We can count on his presence no matter what comes our way.

The Perseverance of Paul and Silas

Throughout the Bible, we find examples of perseverance in the face of adversity, but I'm particularly drawn to the challenges Paul and Silas faced. They were traveling extensively and teaching people about the good news of God's grace. At one point in the city of Philippi, they encountered a slave who earned her master a great deal of money through fortune telling. This woman followed Paul and Silas around for several days and announced their arrival at every turn.

The Bible says, *"Finally Paul became so annoyed that he turned around and said to the spirit, "In the name of Jesus Christ I command you to come out of her!" At that moment the spirit left her." (Acts 16:18 – NIV)*

It's funny to see that Paul's humanity (being annoyed) motivated the expulsion of this demon. As you can imagine, her owners weren't too happy about the fact that she could no longer tell fortunes, because the demon was long gone. They riled up quite a crowd and accused Paul and Silas of advocating customs unlawful for Romans to practice.

"The crowd joined in the attack against Paul and Silas, and the magistrates ordered them to be stripped and beaten with rods. After they had been severely flogged, they were thrown into prison, and the jailer was commanded to guard them carefully. When he received these orders, he put them in the inner cell and fastened their feet in the stocks." (Acts 16:22-24 – NIV)

Stripped naked. Beaten with rods. Flogged with sharp objects attached to the end of a whip. Shackled and placed in an interior cell so that they couldn't escape.

All of a sudden, the beating my staff took at Narsipatnam seems like nothing.

"About midnight Paul and Silas were praying and singing hymns to God, and the other prisoners were listening to them. Suddenly there was such a violent earthquake that the foundations of the prison were shaken. At once all the prison doors flew open, and everyone's chains came loose. The jailer woke up, and when he saw the prison doors open, he drew his sword and was

about to kill himself because he thought the prisoners had escaped." (Acts 16:25-27 – NIV)

In that day, a jailer staked his honor (and ultimately his life) on the fact he could keep an inmate locked up in prison. Notice that when the jailer is faced with adversity (the apparent escape of Paul and Silas), he decides it would be more expedient to commit suicide than be put to death by his superiors.

The jailer quickly moves toward extreme apprehension (fear) in the face of challenge.

"But Paul shouted, "Don't harm yourself! We are all here! The jailer called for lights, rushed in and fell trembling before Paul and Silas. He then brought them out and asked, "Sirs, what must I do to be saved?" (Acts 6:28-30 – NIV)

Paul and Silas shared about the grace of God through Jesus Christ as the jailer bandaged up their wounds, and the jailer's entire household chose to follow Jesus and were immediately baptized – in the middle of the night! Not only did the jailer bring them to his home, but he prepared a meal for them.

The result – *"He was filled with joy because he had come to believe in God - he and his whole household." (Acts 16:34 – NIV)*

In the midst of adversity, Paul and Silas could have easily moved toward aggression or apprehension. Instead, they chose to press on in three profound ways that both challenge and inspire me:

1. **They pressed on by praising God.**

   Paul and Silas were undoubtedly in great pain from the physical beating and flogging. I can't even imagine the physical and mental torment they had just gone through. Instead of asking God "why" or blaming God for getting them into this mess, they were praying and singing songs to Him.

   In moments when we'd rather pick up the phone and vent to a friend or open up Facebook and post our frustration, what would happen if we turned our attention to God? What would happen if we popped in our ear buds and listened to songs that tell of the greatness of God? Praising Him in moments of adversity reminds us that He's always present, all-knowing, and all-powerful.

COMPELLED

Since 2008, Harvest India has been operating on 50% of our normal budget, because our donors in the West have been experiencing financial challenges during the recession. It is only by the grace of God we've been able to continue caring for over 1,300 orphans in our children's homes during this time.

Since the very beginning, we've scheduled morning and evening sessions of worship and prayer for all the children and staff at every home. We gather and sing songs of praise to God – thanking Him for all He has done in our lives.

We're pressing on by praising God.

Our devout Hindu auditor is amazed at the work we're able to accomplish, and he asked me, "How are you running such a huge ministry with such little money? Every project continues to move forward, but the finances are so low."

I respond, "I'm not doing it. Jesus is multiplying our resources like He did with the two fish and five loaves."

After I recounted the story of Jesus feeding the 5,000, our auditor considered the story in light of our situation, "That's very interesting. I'll have to think about that."

Even now in the midst of political infighting and civil unrest in the state of Andhra Pradesh, most all our supplies are 50% more expensive. As we praise God in the midst of adversity, He gives us wisdom on how to wisely use the resources He provides. Instead of giving the kids meat twice a week, we feed them more vegetables and eggs. We cut down on ministry travel to remote villages, host fewer medical camps, put on only one crusade a year (instead of four or five), and eliminate recreational activities for our staff.

When we're faced with any type of challenge (whether financial, physical, or relational), we can easily move toward anger or fear – or we can press on by praising God. The truth is that God will never let us down. Whatever battle you're going through belongs to the Lord. Learn from the example of Paul and Silas. There's no need for you to fight it. Start praising Him – knowing that He's fighting on your behalf.

2. They pressed on with a positive attitude.

The Bible tells us the feet of Paul and Silas were placed in stocks, and many assume their hands were also shackled to prevent them from using their arms. Can you imagine how difficult it must have been to sit or even lay down with their wounds and these physical restraints?

These two faithful men set out to share "good news" with people who were in need of God's saving grace, and instead, they are beaten by an angry mob. This wasn't just a dirty look by their co-workers in the lunch-room for talking about Jesus. We're talking about a physical encounter that would make many utter the words, "I quit."

How easy it is to become selfish in the midst of suffering!

I understand that the Bible doesn't capture every word in the midst of their ordeal, but I don't hear any complaining going on in that dark, interior jail cell. As I listen in on this ancient conversation, I hear words of encouragement. I believe Paul saw this as an opportunity to serve.

"God has called us to something great."
"Jesus wouldn't give up in this moment, and we can't either."
"Let's trust that God is at work in ways that we can't see in this moment."

By choosing to have a positive attitude in moments of adversity, we're more likely to experience a positive outcome. Notice I said that it's a "choice". When challenges come our way, we need to acknowledge our feelings in the moment, and choose our attitude – the way we are going to think about something. I may not feel like having a good attitude, but by making a conscious choice to have a positive outlook on the situation, my feelings usually catch up sooner than later.

I'm reminded of Srinu – a 14-year-old boy with no education who was brought to the Harvest India campus by one of our pastors, because his parents were too poor to care for him. My family took him in as a foster child, because he would have had such a difficult time fitting in with the other children who were so far ahead of him in school.

One day while doing some chores, he collapses on the ground, and we rush him to the hospital. The doctor diagnoses him with a heart problem and instructs us to take him to a specialist. We immediately drive him to the hospital in Vijiwada an hour away, and they find four holes in his heart.

The doctors are shocked that Srinu has been living with this condition, and they indicate heart surgery is needed within 24 hours at a cost of $8,000.

Talk about adversity! Where am I going to find that kind of money?

It could have been so easy to be filled with fear or anger in this moment. Even though I didn't ask for this kid to be dropped off at our campus, I love every foster child as if they were my own.

"We can do this," I tell my wife, Christina. "I don't know how, but I am 100% confident God will provide."

After leaving Srinu at the hospital for further observation, we arrive back in Tenali for dinner with a visiting team of five people from the Netherlands.

"Suresh, what's going on? What happened?" their leader asks.

"One of my foster children needs surgery for his heart, or he's going to die," I inform them. "I just don't know where we're going to come up with $8,000."

Even though I am filled with faith, my mind is scanning through all the options trying to figure out how to save Srinu's life. I'm pacing back and forth – praying – talking to my team – and crying out to God. As the visiting team huddles in prayer, I find myself overwhelmed with thankfulness for their presence, but nothing could have prepared me for their generosity.

"We will take care of it. We will pay for Srinu's surgery."
My eyes well up with tears, and I embrace each one of them in disbelief.

Cristina and I with Srinu after his recovery

The very next day, Srinu made it through eight hours of surgery, and he fully recovered. In fact, he went on to graduate from Bible college, married a beautiful young woman, and he is pastoring a church in Sundaraya Colony.

In moments like these, I have a keen awareness that my tongue is connected to my attitude. If I focus on the adversity and allow negativity to consume my thoughts, I will miss out on what God is trying to do around me. If I choose to focus on God's unwavering character and fill my mind and mouth with words of hope, my outlook changes. I may not even feel what I'm saying in the moment. Yet, I believe the words are true, and I know they will impact my heart.

"God, you are greater than any problem I'll ever face."
"I am a child of God, and You have a great plan for my life."
"I'm not sure what You are doing in this situation, but I know You have it handled."

Can you feel the difference? Just by uttering those positive, hope-filled words, your attitude can change, and your feelings are sure to follow. It's really up to you.

3. They pressed on with grace and forgiveness.

As we read in Acts 16, there was such a violent earthquake that all the chains fell off Paul, Silas, and the other prisoners, and the doors to the prison were busted open. The interior cell must have been quite dark, because the jailer couldn't see the men inside and simply assumed they had escaped.

I'm not sure why Paul and Silas didn't jump to their feet and run out the door. Perhaps, there wasn't enough time or they were too injured or they wanted to honor the authorities. Or, maybe, God kept them there for the specific purpose of saving the life of the jailer. Not only did they prevent him from committing suicide, but they also shared about the saving grace of Jesus.

This jailer was the man who was holding them captive. He was the one who was enforcing the order of the magistrates. I'm sure he watched them being beaten, and he may have even done some of the whipping himself. Out of aggression or apprehension, Paul and Silas could have easily watched him end his life and stepped over the body on the way out of prison.

Instead, they extended grace.

That's the only explanation for their willingness to save his life and tell him about Jesus. Can you imagine being stripped naked, whipped repeatedly, shackled in jail, saving the jailer's life, and leading him to Jesus – all within 24 hours?

I believe the only reason why they were able to forgive their captor is because they recognized how much they had been forgiven themselves. People who have gratitude in their hearts for God's incredible gift of grace tend to be those most willing to dispense that grace to others in the midst of adversity.

As I mentioned earlier, in 2001 when we purchased 20 acres of farmland for $42,000 right outside of Tenali, we were so excited to develop it as a hub for Harvest India. After closing the deal, we got word from other bidders that the land was sold at such a cheap price, because there was no water in the ground.

This was a small detail the seller's did not disclose.

Farmers had been irrigating their crops with water from a nearby canal fed by the Krishna River, and local homes were using water tanks. Because of the amount of water we would need for our facilities, we knew that these options would never work for us.

Should we get angry at the seller?
Should we try to get our money back?
Should we take him to court and sue?

No, we extended grace, and we prayed.

We've supplied over 800 water wells in rural villages.

> For seven days, we cried out to God – asking for the miracle of water to flow from that ground. On the seventh day, a drilling company bored down 120 feet, and water started to flow immediately.
>
> We cheered with excitement, and both the seller and the other bidders were shocked. Now, over 600 people live on that property and enjoy the water coming from the same well. It's amazing how liberating grace can be. When we choose to forgive those who have wronged us in the midst of adversity, something supernatural begins to flow from the depths of our lives. Let it flow.

When I share these stories, I know some people simply write me off as having a simple-minded, third world faith. Maybe in your heart, you've even said, "That stuff could never happen where I live." The only way you'll find out is if you ask God to open up your mind and heart.

Call me simple-minded, but I *do* believe.

I have tasted and seen the goodness of the Lord, and I want nothing else. That's why I'm willing to persevere in the face of adversity, because I know that my God will supply all my needs. I have seen Him do it time after time. I know I serve a supernatural God whose wonder-working power is unleashed when I put my faith and trust in Him.

The same can be true for you.

God has been incredibly good to you already, but He has even better things planned for you now. Now is the season when He wants to move mountains in your life. Put your mustard seed of faith in Him, and press on toward the prize that awaits you. Will you persevere?

SMALL GROUP WEEK #8

Getting Started

1. Who do you admire in recent history who has persevered to overcome adversity? What is it about that person that is attractive to you?

2. In your own words, define adversity and perseverance.

3. What are the pitfalls of responding to adversity through…

   a. Aggression?

   b. Apprehension?

Going Deeper

4. Read Acts 16:16-39. What are you most amazed by, and why?

5. In Paul and Silas' moments of darkness, why do you think they chose to praise God?

6. Can you imagine being beaten, placed in stocks, and thrown into a dark jail? Why do you think Paul and Silas didn't just quit?

7. Paul and Silas could have let the jailer kill himself. Why do you think they stopped him?

Applying It To Your Life

8. In the midst of adversity, what is most difficult for you to do, and why?

   a. Press on by praising God.
   b. Press on with a positive attitude.
   c. Press on with grace and forgiveness.

9. As you think about your own life, where are you tempted to give up? Where do you need to persevere?

10. What action step do you need to take in order to persevere?

CHAPTER 9

I AM COMPELLED TO BRING PEOPLE FROM DARKNESS TO LIGHT

Several years ago, Shakeena was begging all alone. With a tattered sari wrapped around her frail frame, she shuffled along the busy streets of Tenali – roaming here and there – trying to find a willing soul to drop a few rupees in her gnarled hands.

After her husband passed away, none of her adult children wanted to take her in, and she was left to fend for herself – something that's all too common in India. As you can imagine, no one wanted to hire an elderly woman – even for the most menial of tasks.

As she went about her daily begging, a local shop owner told her about our elderly home in town, but Shakeena was leery to approach us for help. She was a Muslim. For months, she barely survived on the handouts she received on her long walks. With no more strength to continue this way of life, she finally faced her fear and approached one of our staff members.

"I am old and can not take care of myself. I need food and a place to live."

"We will be glad to help you," said the manager of our elderly home.

"But…I am a Muslim, and you are a Christian organization," Shakeena replied with her head hanging low. "Why would you help me?"

He calmed her fears and ushered her in the front door – explaining that the home welcomes anyone who is in need. Still leery about the offer of assistance, she slowly warmed up to the other elderly residents as she enjoyed the food, shelter, clothing, and medicine we provided.

The one thing she didn't warm up to – was Jesus.

In all our children and elderly homes, we share the teachings of Jesus and invite the young and old to join us in following Him. While most are strongly attracted to the love they experience in our homes, Shakeena had no interest in Christianity. She was a strong, devout Muslim – devoted to her faith. We didn't push her, because we trust that God's love shines through.

What we don't often realize is that God's love shines brightest in some of the darkest moments of life.

For Shakeena, that dark moment came in the midst of sickness, which prevented her from even getting out of bed to go to the bathroom. Because I've never been in that situation, I can only imagine the feelings of utter powerlessness she felt in those moments. As our staff cleaned up the diarrhea she was laying in, she couldn't believe they were willing to help her. She was overwhelmed by love.

"I am not your mother or your close friend. Why are you doing this for me? Even my own children neglect me."

It's one thing to hear about the teachings of Jesus, but it's quite another to experience His love firsthand in the midst of our own frailty. As Shakeena started to cry, our staff reminded her, "We're doing this for you because of Jesus. He died for you and gave his life. He said to take care of people in need, and that's why we welcomed you into the home."

"What if I want Jesus in *my* life?" she asked.

On that day – having just been cleaned – Shakeena chose to follow Jesus.

"When I die, I don't want to be buried like a Muslim. I want to be buried as a Christian." She repeated these words over and over to our staff in the days to come, because she was so grateful for the love of Jesus she experienced in the home. Just a few weeks ago, Shakeena passed away, and we celebrated her life as a follower of Jesus – just like she wanted.

Would we have continued to love and care for Shakeena if she never chose to follow Jesus? Absolutely! Because we are called to love our neighbor and look after widows and orphans in their distress. Yet, Jesus calls us to make disciples, and we believe that God's love shines so brightly that it naturally leads people out of the darkness they are walking in.

Pastor Prakash (left) and I leading a time of prayer.

In India, there are so many gods being worshipped that Jesus is just another deity to add to the long list. If we proclaim, "Jesus is Lord" and do not demonstrate His love through our lives, then we are simply talking into the wind.

We have found that we're most effective in ministry when we are centered on three simple words uttered by a man named William Booth – "soup, soap, and salvation."

In 1865, William Booth, an ordained Methodist minister, formed a group focused on preaching among the unchurched people living in the midst of abject poverty in London's East End. Early on, he recognized the need for a holistic approach that addressed a person's material, emotional and spiritual needs. In addition to preaching the Good News of Jesus Christ, Booth started providing food and shelter for the needy and rehabilitation for alcoholics.

Booth knew that words without deeds would be fruitless, and he embraced his now-famous strategy encapsulated in three words.

Soup, Soap, and Salvation

By "soup", he meant meeting the physical needs of the poor through food, shelter, job training, and work programs.

By "soap", he recognized a person's need for cleanliness - an essential for dignity and self-confidence.

And then we have "salvation". Booth famously said, "No one gets a blessing if they have cold feet, and nobody ever got saved while they had toothache!"

Through the power of "soup, soap, and salvation", Harvest India has been bringing people from darkness to light for many years.

You Are the Light of the World

Throughout the Scriptures, the symbols of light and darkness are used to convey a revolutionary spiritual shift. The metaphor is incredibly powerful to those living in rural India, because they know how important light truly is.

Imagine yourself working late in the fields during harvest season – far from your hut. As the sun begins to dip below the horizon, you realize that all the other workers have jumped on their bikes to head home. You find yourself all alone on the edge of the field needing to wind your way back down the long path.

In the midst of the darkness, your arm brushes up against the sharp branches of the surrounding trees, and you wince in pain. Soon, you stumble and fall over rocks on the path as you hear the sounds of an approaching wild boar. In fear, you start to run, but you've lost your way. You don't know which direction is home.

Darkness prevents us from finding our way Home.

It blinds us from seeing the truth about ourselves, about life, and about God. It impairs our judgment and tricks us into thinking sin is going to fulfill that deep-down longing inside each one of us. It causes us to become suspicious of others and creates fear in our hearts.

God knew we couldn't find our way out of the darkness on our own, so He sent Jesus to walk among us and open our eyes to the light. Jesus says, *"I am the light of the world. Whoever follows me will never walk in darkness, but will have the light of life." (John 8:12 – NIV)*

Notice that Jesus says you will "have the light of life" if you follow Him. Not only does this light open your eyes to the fact that you are loved by Him, but it gives you the ability to shine a light on the path for others who are trying to find their way out of their own darkness.

Our lives are like a giant spiritual flashlight guiding people toward Home.

In fact, Jesus says, *"You are the light of the world. A town built on a hill cannot be hidden. Neither do people light a lamp and put it under a bowl. Instead they put it on its stand, and it gives light to everyone in the house. In the same way, let your light shine before others, that they may see your good deeds and glorify your Father in heaven." (Matthew 5:14-16 – NIV)*

One of the most powerful ways we let our light shine before others is through our good deeds. Think back to Shakeena. She heard about Jesus and His teachings, but it wasn't until someone loved her in a moment of darkness that she experienced the Light herself.

Do you realize most people don't even recognize they're walking in darkness? They think stumbling through life – trying to find meaning and purpose – is just normal. People are searching for their identity in all sorts of things that only leave them feeling unfulfilled and even more empty. When you're walking in darkness, the main thing you're focused on is yourself. Light opens your eyes – and your heart – to the fact that God has a much bigger plan for each one of us.

Listen as the apostle Paul recounts his first encounter with the Light. *"I saw a light from heaven, brighter than the sun, blazing around me and my companions." Jesus said to him, "I am sending you to…open their eyes and turn them from darkness to light, and from the power of Satan to God, so that they may receive forgiveness of sins and a place among those who are sanctified by faith in me." (Acts 26:13,17-18 – NIV)*
Through a supernatural encounter, Paul – one who was walking in darkness but now enveloped in a heavenly light – was being sent out into the world to guide people toward Home. Can you imagine? One minute he's walking in darkness trying to stomp out this burgeoning movement of Christ-followers. The next minute – his entire life is illuminated by the Light of Christ. His eyes are opened to life as it was intended to be lived – in the light of God's love.

Unique Challenges in the West
If you haven't picked up on it already, this whole concept of helping people move from darkness to light is commonly called "evangelism" among Christians. I fully recognize this subject can be disconcerting for many in the West. Because spirituality and faith are a regular part of everyday life in India, evangelism is something we do out in the open on a regular basis. We lead through acts of service, but we're always faithful to share God's Word and the love of Jesus to point people toward the Light.

In the West, I've learned that many feel guilty for not sharing their faith "enough", and others feel too embarrassed to share their faith at all. I'm wondering if this might be why:

TO BRING PEOPLE FROM DARKNESS TO LIGHT

1. I'm embarrassed to be one of *those* Christians.

Perhaps, you grew up in a church where you were taught a particular method of evangelism, and you were challenged to "win" a certain number of people to Christ. Maybe you were given tracts emblazoned with burning flames to hand out to friends, or maybe you were encouraged to invite people to events or movies that warned of the impending doom. Did these things scare you or turn you off in some way?

Truth: People don't want to be your project, but they do want to be loved. What if you genuinely want the best for the people around you? What if Jesus really has lit up your life in a way that you're experiencing His love, peace, and joy? Wouldn't that be pretty amazing if your family and friends could experience that, too?

2. I'm worried about doing it the *right* way.

Have you heard your pastor talk about evangelism in a way that made you feel like you need to be a super-Christian in order know all the right Scriptures to recite? Are you scared you won't know how to answer someone's question? Or, do you think you need to be farther along in your faith before you share about God?

Truth: God can use anyone to share His love with another human being. Yes, we can all be growing in our knowledge of the Bible, but God wants us to use the understanding and experiences we have right now. He is not limited by our limitations.

3. Religion is a *personal* subject.

With religion and politics as such taboo subjects, face-to-face conversations about these things are few and far between – often regarded as "personal". While both topics may be the source of constant chatter online as people try to convince one another to adopt another belief, there's something much more intimate about discussing one's faith while looking into the eyes of another human being.

Truth: People need a safe place to process their faith. Rather than coming with all the "answers", what if you started asking questions? What if your genuine curiosity created a healthy environment to talk about their beliefs about God?

4. God wouldn't want to use *me*.

Maybe you discount God's desire to use you to bring someone from darkness to light. Are you feeling guilty about past behaviors before choosing to follow Jesus? Are you worried that your current imperfections disappoint God in some way? Do you feel like you have to live a perfect life in order to introduce people to a perfect God?

Truth: None of us are perfect in our attitudes or actions. That's the whole reason why we need God's grace. When we're honest with our shortcomings, His grace is incredibly attractive to people who are searching for hope in their lives. God not only can use you, but He wants to use you!

Notice that the four objections to sharing our faith seem to flow from feelings of inadequacy, but I'm not sure that's the real reason why we don't point people toward Jesus. I'm wondering if it's more about a spiritual deadness in our own lives.

Think about it this way.

If something or someone has deeply touched my life, it's quite likely that I'm going to tell you about it. When you see a movie that inspires you, do you recommend it to others? When you go to a new restaurant and have a wonderful experience, aren't you talking about it the next day? If someone goes above and beyond to help you, don't you rave about it to your friends and family?

So, here's what I'm wondering.

Could it be that we're not in touch with our own brokenness?
Could it be that we've lost sight of the magnitude of God's grace?
Could it be that we've grown cold to God's love?

I'm not trying to push you into mustering up the courage to share your faith. I'm more interested in directing your eyes to His light so that your life will be all consumed by His love.

As Paul writes, *"Remember, our Message is not about ourselves; we're proclaiming Jesus Christ, the Master. All we are is messengers, errand runners from Jesus for you. It started when God said, "Light up the darkness!" and our lives filled up with light as we saw and understood God in the face of Christ, all bright and beautiful." (2 Corinthians 4:5-6 – MSG)*

It is when we experience the beauty and majesty of Jesus that we're compelled to guide people toward Home.

Loving, Not Selling

Recently, India has imported a business strategy in the West called MLM – multi-level marketing. While I'm always happy for people to find creative ways to provide for their families, I'm very intrigued by the methods by which products are sold. My guess is you've had someone try to enroll you in a business for your benefit, but you soon start to sense that it's more about him or her in some way.

Let's get this straight.
Jesus didn't call us to *sell* Christianity.
He calls us to *love* the world.

Your co-worker doesn't want to be your target, but everyone wants to be loved. Your family doesn't want love with strings attached, but they do need your help. Your neighbors don't want to be "won" to Christ, but they do need meaning and purpose in their lives.

I'm way more concerned about our *motive* for bringing people from darkness to light rather than our *methods*. The apostle Paul makes it ever so clear that love is the key to everything.

"If I speak with human eloquence and angelic ecstasy but don't love, I'm nothing but the creaking of a rusty gate. If I speak God's Word with power, revealing all his mysteries and making everything plain as day, and if I have faith that says to a mountain, "Jump," and it jumps, but I don't love, I'm nothing. If I give everything I own to the poor and even go to the stake to be burned as a martyr, but I don't love, I've gotten nowhere. So, no matter what I say, what I believe, and what I do, I'm bankrupt without love." (1 Corinthians 13:1-3 - MSG)

When we are passionately following Jesus and our lives are fully engulfed in His light, we become a conduit through which His love is dispensed to the world.

Although I will share several practical ways to bring people from darkness to light, I've found that these two things are more important than anything else:

- **Embrace how much you're loved by Jesus.**

  The Bible makes it incredibly clear that God is love. All His motives, actions, and words are rooted in the fact that He is loving.

  "This is how God showed his love among us: He sent his one and only Son into the world that we might live through him. This is love: not that we loved God, but that he loved us and sent his Son as an atoning sacrifice for our sins. Dear friends, since God so loved us, we also ought to love one another." (1 John 4:9-11 - NIV)

  Right now, God loves you fully and completely. Why? Because He created you, and you belong to Him. You are His child, and He has gone to enormous lengths to express His love to you through the life and death of Jesus Christ.

  It may sound a bit childish, but maybe we need to get back in touch with the child-like wonder that comes with singing "Jesus Love Me."

  Jesus loves me,
  This I know,
  For the Bible tells me so.
  Little ones to Him belong;
  They are weak, but He is strong.

  Yes, Jesus loves me!
  Yes, Jesus loves me!
  Yes, Jesus loves me!
  The Bible tells me so.

  There's something about the simplicity of that song that helps me embrace the reality that Jesus loved me enough to step out of heaven and show us a new way of life – a life of love.

- **Cultivate an undying love for humanity.**

  If Jesus is all about love – and we are His followers, shouldn't we be all about love, too? Yet, somehow, we get sidetracked with being the morality police for the world or fighting about what type of music to play in our churches.

God created everyone, and He loves everyone.
He loves Pakistanis as much as He loves Indians.
He cares about Afghanistan as much as He cares about America.

Every person on this planet has a story that includes hopes, dreams, fears, frustrations, and failures, and they didn't choose which family they would be born into. No matter where they live or what language they speak, they are more like you than they are different.

We're all spinning on this enormous ball we call planet Earth, and we all desperately want to be loved. In fact, we are hard-wired to receive love and give love.

Jesus is not a product, and we're not selling a membership to an exclusive club. Jesus is our leader, and His agenda can be summed up in one word – love. As you're embracing His love for you, then you're ready to start sharing it with others.

Three Ways to Shine Your Light

After being honest with some unique Western challenges and re-focusing on love as our central motive, now we're ready to look at three ways we can help people move from darkness to light. These are not theoretical in any way. These are central to how I live and how Harvest India has helped thousands of people choose to follow Jesus.

1. Take compelling action on behalf of others.

The weight of daily responsibilities combined with the fast pace of life can grind us down to the point that we have little margin to do much more than simply survive. The combination of earning a living, raising kids, and dealing with unexpected problems can lull us into living an average life.

In the midst of it all, you have the *choice* how you will act. You choose your behaviors and responses every single day. What would it look like to start taking compelling action on behalf of others?

COMPELLED

Instead of avoiding the darkness in other people's lives, what if you saw yourself as a source of His light? Remember what it's like to be stumbling around in the dark trying to find your way in life. Can you imagine how alone that feels?

Compelling action – motivated by love – looks like meeting your neighbors and knowing them by name (something quite extraordinary in many neighborhoods). What if you started tuning in to the challenges in the lives of your co-workers or classmates? Instead of telling them what they should do (or judging them by your own standards), what if you listened to them, shared what you've learned in your own life, and found practical ways to help them? What if you started going out of your way to say "yes" when people are in need rather than just turning your head?

Several years ago for my birthday, I announced on Facebook that I would be honored if people would donate money toward a water well. Within a short amount of time, generous friends donated $1,200 needed, and we traveled to Mothadaka - a village of Muslims and Hindus who had been walking for miles to get their water. When we shared our desire to give them a water well, they told us that only salt water was coming from the ground. In this midst of this discouraging news, we approached a strong Hindu family and asked them to share a small piece of land so we could drill a well for the entire village.

This was compelling action in the face of their great need.

As we prayed for clean water, we had no idea that the couple took compelling action themselves. The husband and wife said to one another, "If these Christians pray and their God grants good water, we will give them all our land."

While we were drilling the well to 150 feet, God answered our prayers for clean drinking water, and the entire village was shocked. Our compelling action caused this couple to be compelled to give us the deed to a quarter of an acre – their entire property, and they both became followers of Jesus. Not only is there a water well for the entire village, but we're now building a church and elderly home on the property.

What if your love for humanity compelled you to take action on behalf of those who are in darkness? I wonder what God might do.

2. Pray compelling prayers.

As a follower of Jesus, the Holy Spirit is living within you – the same Spirit that raised Christ from the dead. You have direct access to call upon the Spirit at any moment in time. Can you believe you have something that powerful inside you?

Paul goes so far to say, *"In the same way, the Spirit helps us in our weakness. We do not know what we ought to pray for, but the Spirit himself intercedes for us through wordless groans." (Romans 8:26 – NIV)*

There are people in your life who need the power of God to give them wisdom, guidance, comfort, and healing, and He has invited us to ask him for such things.

Jesus taught, *"Which of you, if your son asks for bread, will give him a stone? Or if he asks for a fish, will give him a snake? If you, then, though you are evil, know how to give good gifts to your children, how much more will your Father in heaven give good gifts to those who ask him!" (Matthew 7:9-11 - NIV)*

You know family, friends, and co-workers who are having marital problems, health issues, child-rearing challenges, or some other struggles. What if you started praying for them? What if you actually asked to pray for them in person? I wonder how God might use that interaction to intervene in their life and draw them out of darkness and into the light of His love.

Five years ago, Sarada, a neighbor down the street, started to notice people coming to and from our home to get food, medical help, and even money for coffin boxes for deceased family members. As a local Hindu priest's wife, Sarada felt the need to come over and share her opinion with my wife, "You are going against karma. Those people deserve the life they are living, because of what they did in their past lives."

Christina didn't argue with her, but she shared many stories about Jesus' love for people in need. There was something about the interaction that prompted the woman to come back the next day to continue the conversation. Meanwhile, Christina was praying for Sarada to see the light of God's love.

On the second day, the woman noticed, "When people come over to your home, they are sad, but when they leave, they have a smile on their face. At the temple, I never see anyone smiling."

Speaking in words that Sarada could understand, Christina shared, "We do not worship Jesus out of fear. We are here to change bad karma to good karma through God's love."

After a long pause, Christina asked, "Would you like me to pray for you?"

Resistance to the message of Jesus was now gone, because Sarada had experienced love in our home, the smiles of those we serve, and now the power of prayer to give her comfort. She had been wrestling with the reality of giving money and praying prayers at the temple, but it was motivated by fear. When she started coming to our home, she began to experience His love. She even went so far as to ask Christina to teach her to pray – on her second visit to our home!

As she returned for another visit on the third day, Sarada asked, "If I want to follow Jesus, what do I do?"

Christina knew she needed a compelling next step that would propel her into the light. "If you want to follow Jesus, you can't go to the temple and worship any other gods. You'll need to devote your life to the one true God."

What you may not realize is that she was living on the temple campus with her husband, the Hindu priest. After choosing to follow Jesus, it took Sarada several weeks to share her decision with her husband and family. The result - the entire family chose to follow Jesus and moved off the temple campus. In fact, Sarada still comes by our home every few weeks to pray with Christina.

You have access to something powerful, and the people around you need it. Remember, your life is a flashlight pointing the way toward Home in the midst of the darkness.

We baptize people in nearby rivers after they follow Jesus.

3. Use compelling words.

In everything we do through Harvest India, we always start with "soup" and "soap" – meeting physical needs of people, and we pray for God to demonstrate His love through mighty miracles.

In the process, we speak compelling words – His Word – into their lives.

We firmly believe that Jesus is the only one who can lead a person from the kingdom of darkness to the Kingdom of God, but we have been given the privilege of speaking on His behalf.

Paul writes, *"We are therefore Christ's ambassadors, as though God were making his appeal through us. We implore you on Christ's behalf: Be reconciled to God." (2 Corinthians 5:20 - NIV)*

As Christ's ambassadors in India, we go to extreme lengths to speak compelling words of faith to people who have never heard of Jesus. Beyond our day-to-day ministries, there are times when we identify a town that has many villages in the surrounding area, and we rent out a large field to host a multi-night crusade.

In order to help people get to and from the event, we hire rickshaws, trucks, and tractors with flatbed trailers to pick up as many people as possible in the villages. Over the years, thousands of people have chosen to follow Jesus by hearing God's Word presented through song, dance, drama, and preaching.

Although every crusade is profound, the event we hosted in 2008 in Suryapet – about 5 hours away – truly stands out in my mind. After two months of planning, we experienced an incredible time of prayer on the opening night of the four-day crusade.

A high-caste Hindu man who had been crippled and unable to walk for many years was brought to the event on a cot. As we prayed for him, the man slowly rose to his feet and began to take one small step after another. Not only did he walk across the stage, but he walked all the way back to his home. Because he was well known in the town, many people heard about the miracle and came to the crusade.

I realize that this is hard to understand in the West. We pray for God to do miracles every day, and oftentimes He chooses to change someone's life in an instant.

During the next three nights, over 100,000 people attended the crusade, and 26,000 people chose to follow Jesus while many deaf and blind were healed on the spot – with their families standing by to verify the miracles. The family of the Hindu man who was dramatically healed ended up choosing to follow Jesus as well, and they donated a piece of property for a church to be built. These people had been worshipping gods out of *fear*, but they experienced Jesus being worshipped out of *love*.

Although you may have an opportunity to invite a friend to a special church service or crusade from time to time, the most compelling words that can be spoken into his or her life are the words that come from you.

What if you were courageous enough to start spiritual conversations with a genuine interest in the beliefs of another? What if you were willing to share your own story of faith in a way that's truly vulnerable and heart-felt? What if you weren't worried about trying to convince them of something and deeply cared about what's going on in their life?

TO BRING PEOPLE FROM DARKNESS TO LIGHT

Your words can be compelling. The question is - what are they compelling people toward?

The truth is that many in India need to encounter the light of Jesus for the first time, but the West is in need of revival. The gospel is accessible everywhere you look – via TV, radio, books, churches, and the Internet, but many people aren't even interested.

Most don't even realize they are walking around in darkness until they stumble into a pit of despair when life doesn't turn out as they had envisioned – the loss of a job, the death of a loved one, a health scare, or any other mid-life crisis. It's in those moments of darkness when the light of God's love can shine brightest, and people are more willing to open their eyes to see life from a new perspective.

The apostle Paul reminds us, *"Everyone who calls on the name of the Lord will be saved." How, then, can they call on the one they have not believed in? And how can they believe in the one of whom they have not heard? And how can they hear without someone preaching to them? And how can anyone preach unless they are sent? As it is written: "How beautiful are the feet of those who bring good news!" (Romans 10:13-15 - NIV)*

Your feet are bringing good news – a beautiful message of love to the world, and your life has the power to illuminate the path for others to find their way Home.

What would it look like for you to shine brightly?

SMALL GROUP WEEK #9

Getting Started

1. When you were a kid, were you scared of the dark? If so, did you do anything to overcome your fears?

2. Read John 8:12. What can "darkness" represent spiritually? (Think beyond sin to other concepts as well.)

Going Deeper

3. Read Acts 26:9-18 to hear Paul share his story with King Agrippa. As you look at the calling on Paul's life (verses 17-18), do you think other followers of Jesus have the same calling? Why or why not?

4. What's the difference between selling Christianity and sharing what Jesus has done in our lives?

5. To ensure we are "loving not selling", Suresh invites us to…

   a. Embrace how much you're loved by Jesus.
   b. Cultivate an undying love for humanity.

   Why are those two things so important to develop healthy motives as we share our faith?

Applying It To Your Life

6. As you think about your own life, what do you think prevents you from sharing your faith more?

   a. I'm embarrassed to be one of those Christians.
   b. I'm worried about doing it the right way.
   c. Religion is a personal subject.
   d. God wouldn't want to use me.

7. How does the idea of "lighting the path so others can find their way Home" help you think about evangelism in a fresh way?

8. Three ways to "shine your light" are discussed:

a. Take compelling action on behalf of others.
b. Pray compelling prayers.
c. Use compelling words.

Which one is hardest for you, and why? Which one is easiest?

9. As you think about the people in your life, who do you genuinely love that is stumbling around in darkness? How do you sense God is leading you to be a light in their life?

CHAPTER 10

I AM COMPELLED TO SAVE, SHEPHERD, AND SEND OUT THE NEXT GENERATION

Each time I visit Harvest India's partners in the West, I have the opportunity to spend time in many of their homes, and I'm greeted with hugs and kisses and words of support from adults and children alike. There's something incredibly personal about stepping into the living space of another family. I get the opportunity to experience their culture, family rituals, and personal values in a way that goes beyond mere conversation.

When you step into a family's home, you have the opportunity to step into their lives.

During my first trip to the United States, my eyes were opened to so many fascinating things I had never experienced before. At one home, I was walking down a hallway on my way back from the restroom when I spotted the most peculiar thing – a large, square room with pink walls, flowery curtains, and fancy wooden furniture. The floor of this room was covered in lush carpet, and the ceiling was lit up by a glass chandelier of some sort. There were brightly colored toys lined up along the walls, stuffed animals meticulously arranged on small chairs, and brand new clothes and shoes organized by color in the closet.

My mind was swirling with questions that were too embarrassing to utter to my dinner hosts.

How many children sleep in this extravagant room?
Why are there so many new toys and stuffed animals?
Are all those clothes and shoes for one child?
Why would a child own shoes when they can't even walk yet?
Why is there another bathroom only accessible from inside that pink room?

I tried to put all these questions out of my mind as I made my way back to the dining room, but I eventually pieced everything together.

- This family had a bedroom where only one child (a newborn) slept.
- This baby had her own bathroom – even though she couldn't use it yet.
- The baby's closet was bulging with clothes that had yet to be worn.
- And, there was something farther down the hall called a "play room" - filled with even more toys.

Have you heard of such things?

Where I live in India, I don't know of a single child who has his or her own bedroom, and it would be extremely rare to share a room only with a sibling. In fact, most families in India sleep in the same room. Yes, the entire family.

It is rare for a family to have a mattress; most sleep on raised cots or mats on the floor. Children don't have closets filled with shirts and jeans; they have few sets of clothing on a shelf and one or two pairs of sandals at the most. Most children don't have any toys; that's what sticks and rocks are for. And, no child would ever even imagine having his or her own bathroom; everyone uses the same toilet (aka, hole in the cement floor) out back, and a bath consists of dumping water from the well over your head.

After arriving back in India after my first trip to the US, I thought about starting a "Get Your Child Back in Line" business. I could imagine the brochure, *"Is your child ungrateful for what you've given them? Send them to India for a week or two, and we'll help them appreciate what they have!"* Probably not a good idea.

TO SAVE, SHEPHERD, & SEND OUT THE NEXT GENERATION

Every family I visit in the West is extremely affluent by the standards of our world (roof of their heads, clothes in their closets, food in a refrigerator, and usually one or two vehicles to drive), but most families I work with in India are extremely poor.

There is nothing inherently wrong with having your own bedroom or sleeping with your entire family in the same room. There's nothing bad about having your own restroom or sharing one with everyone. And, there's nothing evil about having a room full of toys or no toys at all.

Yet, in the face of these extreme differences in culture and lifestyle, there are a number of things I think we can all agree every child deserves.

- Shelter to protect him or her from the elements.
- Food and clean drinking water to nourish his or her body.
- Basic clothing to protect his or her body and provide human dignity.
- Access to medical care when in need.
- Access to as much education as they desire.
- A loving family environment where he or she is encouraged.

The way this plays out in the West versus India or anywhere else in the developing world will look quite different. The problem is that many children in India don't have these basic necessities, and it limits their ability to grow up as productive members of a healthy society.

When a child is drinking water from the same river where buffalo are being washed, the possibility of catching diseases increases dramatically. Without access to medical care, infections, loss of limbs, and even death are more likely. Deprived of education, he or she is destined to barely survive by working in the fields. And, without a loving family environment, a child will struggle to develop healthy, meaningful relationships.

Why Is This So Important?
Whether you have kids or not, may I suggest that children are critical to the fabric of our culture and our churches? They are not our *future*; they are our *present!*

Mahatma Gandhi once said, "A nation's greatness is measured by how it treats its weakest members."

Who are the weak in our world?
The sick.
The elderly.
And children.

While some children in the West raise their voices to ask for (or even demand) more things they don't really need, many children in India (and around the globe) have no voice at all.

Children are at the heart of Harvest India's mission.

Children often lack rights, and they are exploited economically through forced labor or commercial sex. They are not seen as human beings with value, and people treat them in ways that cause physical, emotional, and relational damage for years to come. That is not only true in many parts of the world, but it was true in Jesus' day – a time when women and children were not culturally valued. That's why his treatment of both is so shocking to the religious leaders – and even the disciples.

Read what Matthew captures for us, *"At that time the disciples came to Jesus and asked, "Who, then, is the greatest in the kingdom of heaven?" He called a little child to him, and placed the child among them. And he said: "Truly I tell you, unless you change and become like little children, you will never enter the kingdom of heaven. Therefore, whoever takes the lowly position of this child is the greatest in the kingdom of heaven. And whoever welcomes one such child in my name welcomes me." (Matthew 18:1-5 – NIV)*

Can you imagine being that child who Jesus called to come up in front of everyone? My knees would have been knocking! I would have been wondering, "Am I in trouble? What did I do to deserve this?"

Ironically, Jesus pointed out a quality in the child that most of the adults were trying to avoid – being "lowly" or humble. While the disciples were wondering who was going to be the greatest, Jesus was inviting them to be more like the child. In fact, Jesus goes so far to say that they wouldn't enter the kingdom of heaven without becoming like a little one.

Curiosity.
Child-like wonder.
Experiencing the moment.
Not trying to push ahead.
Not worried about status.
Totally dependent.

Finally, Jesus says, *"Whoever welcomes one such child in my name welcomes me."* That's how important children are in the kingdom of God. Jesus likens them to Himself. When we serve children, we're serving Jesus. From the beginning of Harvest India, children have been at the heart of our ministry for three key reasons:

- **Children are loved and valued by God.**

  David writes, *"For you created my inmost being; you knit me together in my mother's womb. I praise you because I am fearfully and wonderfully made; your works are wonderful, I know that full well. My frame was not hidden from you when I was made in the secret place, when I was woven together in the depths of the earth. Your eyes saw my unformed body; all the days ordained for me were written in your book before one of them came to be. How precious to me are your thoughts, God! How vast is the sum of them!" (Psalm 139:13-17 - NIV)*

While many parents in India are unable to or choose not to care for their children for economic reasons, that doesn't change the fact that each child is uniquely created and loved by God. He pays careful attention to the crafting of each little being, and He knows everything about them – even the number of hairs on his or her head.

- **Children will grow up and have families of their own.**

  The way we parent our children has a direct impact on how they develop relationships, who they marry, what their marriage is like, and even how they parent their own children.

  What we model for our children – from the way we talk to how we resolve conflict to the way we treat others – is caught and replicated in their own lives. The way you live your life and lead your family is not only creating your current reality, but it's impacting your child's own family in the years to come.

  If you yell, your child is more likely to yell.
  If you cheat, your child is more likely to cheat.
  If you divorce, your children are more likely to divorce.

  The opposite is true as well.

  If you model loving, encouraging relationships…
  If you honor your spouse with your words and actions…
  If you resolve conflict in healthy ways…
  If you listen to your child and value their thoughts…
  If you love God and follow Jesus authentically…
  If you serve the least, last, and lost…

  Your children will be more likely to do the same.

- **Children are the leaders of tomorrow.**

  The children you and I are raising in our homes will be leading families, businesses, governments, and churches in the days to come. I ask myself, "What type of men and women do I want leading these organizations?"

  My guess is that our answers would be similar.

  I want strong, courageous men and women who are full of faith. I long for our nations to be led by God-fearing people who want to serve – not just be served. I desire leaders who have a heart for the poor and needy and a commitment to take action. I envision leaders who lead by following in the footsteps of Jesus.

  Can you imagine those types of leaders in every facet of our culture? The truth is that children grow up quickly, and they are the leaders of tomorrow. That's why I want to do everything within my power to - *"Start children off on the way they should go, and even when they are old they will not turn from it." (Proverbs 22:6 - NIV)*

These beliefs have shaped our ministry to the children in our area. These are the reasons why we do what we do when it comes to kids. My hope is that you clearly see that these can be your "reasons" for investing in children as well – whether you have kids of your own or not.

Children are precious gifts from God, and we must treat them that way.

Harvest India impacts thousands of children and young adults on a daily basis through our children's homes, schools, and colleges, and we are very focused on training up the next generation. There are three specific strategies we invest in:

Strategy #1: We save children from darkness.

This "saving" comes in the form of rescuing them from abandonment, taking them in when they've been orphaned, and teaching each one about God's love for them.

In 2004 when the tsunami hit the coast of India, it devastated many islands about three hours away from our campus. Most of the homes disappeared, and hundreds of people died within a matter of hours. The only people who survived were the ones who hung on to trees or climbed atop a government-built, cyclone shelter to avoid the flooding.

We traveled by boat to the area and gave away rice, lentils, blankets, fishing nets, stoves, lanterns, utensils, pots, and drinking water – all things lost in the flooding. In the midst of their desperation, the elders of the village began to give us children who were orphaned.

Traveling by boat to outlying islands

The elders would literally walk up to us with children in their arms and ask us to take them with us. They were completely overwhelmed.

Within days, people started dropping children off at our campus as well. Nearly 200 children came from eight islands within a month. One by one – they kept showing up from three hours away. Many were so young they didn't know their own names. Through our government contacts, we were able to give each child new, proper paperwork with an official name and date of birth.

In the midst of the whole ordeal, I kept asking, "Jesus, how are we going to handle all these kids?"

All I know is that God's timing is perfect, and He is gracious and faithful. At the time of the tsunami, we were in the process of constructing a large facility to house 100 children – completely donated by ROCKHARBOR Church in southern California. What we didn't know is the building would ultimately house over 350 children through the creative usage of bunk beds. That building was like Noah's ark for all those children who had lost their families in the flood. Each one of those children was orphaned and alone in the midst of a disaster – a place of serious darkness. Now, they have a new chance at life with all the resources they need.

To handle over 350 children in one location, we have to be extremely organized with their time. Let me lay out their weekly schedule so you can get a feel for what their days are like:

Monday-Saturday

5-6am – Devotions
All of these children come from different religious backgrounds, but most of them were being raised in Hindu homes. If you have children of your own, you know that kids are naturally open to spiritual things and ask many questions about God.

From the beginning of their time with us, we let the children know that God loves them and that He has an amazing plan for their lives. When they experience our love and care for them as well, they are very open to the teachings of Jesus. Because India is such a spiritual place, there is no resistance to the things of God. The children are extremely open to Jesus' love, and they want to participate in worship.

From 5-6am each morning, the entire group gathers on the top floor, and they sing songs, read the Bible, listen to stories, and pray for the needs of our ministry. We're amazed to witness children who are being healed as they pray for one another.

6-8am – Shower and dressed
8am – Breakfast
9am-12noon – School
12-2pm – Lunch
2-4pm – School
4-6pm – Play time and shower

6-7pm – Devotions
7-8pm – Dinner
8-9pm – Elementary homework and studying
8-10pm – High school homework and studying
10pm – Lights out

Sunday

11am-1pm – Church
Because of the number of children, they have their own church service on Sundays. Each child learns two new Scriptures each week, and they memorize the books of the Bible as well. These services are filled with children reciting Bible verses, dancing to Christian music, and teaching from our leaders.

From time to time, we bring in older children (over 10 years of age) who have never gone to school for some reason. Rather than starting them off in first grade and making them feel out of place, we choose not to have them go to school or live in the children's home. Instead, my wife and I take them in as a foster child, and we homeschool them with a basic level of reading and writing so they'll be able to function in the world. Quite a few foster children live with our family and help in the children's home by cleaning, gardening, and carrying wood. I love them like my own children, and they call us Mom and Dad. Almost every one of them goes on to Bible school, gets married, and becomes a pastor.

As you can see, we are extremely committed to saving orphaned and abandoned children from darkness on every level (physically, emotionally, relationally, and spiritually) by providing them with the basic needs of life and the love of Jesus.

Strategy #2: We serve children through education.

Education is the key to helping children break free from the bondage of the caste system. It empowers them to get a quality job and provide for their families. Although most of our 1,300 children attend public school, we do operate one elementary school with 300 children, one high school with 200 children, seven nursing schools, 13 satellite Bible schools, one junior college, and one degree college.

Frankly, I never envisioned we would be doing all this.

For years, all our children went to public school, and they had the opportunity to attend Bible college. If they wanted to do something else, we would try to get them connected as best we could. I didn't want to take a big risk by starting some sort of school we didn't really know about, but God had a different plan.

One day, a Harvest India pastor called me and said, "I just found out about a nursing school that the owners are looking to turn over to another organization if they're willing to pay for it."

Not only was it affordable, but it would allow us to send 60 Dalit girls to nursing college – something they would have never been able to do. After we took over the school, even more girls applied to attend, so the government gave us permission to start more schools. Now, we have five female nursing schools, and two for males.

Nursing students taking their exams

Then, one day out of the blue, a Hindu organization came to us and said, "We would like to give this college to Harvest India." They were having many problems – a lack of unity and a lot of debt with no systematic way to run the school. They were impressed by our ministry and nursing schools, and we had a great reputation from all the awards we've received from the state of Andhra Pradesh.

"We are a Christian organization, and that may be a concern if we run the school like that," I told the Hindu leaders.

"There are no strings attached," they responded. "We just want to place it into good hands."

Three years ago, we started with 500 female students, and KSK College in the Guntur District now has over 1000 students. We hire the best faculty by paying more money to those teachers with a passion for the subject, and we are instilling a strong code of discipline and study.

Many girls are passing with high marks in their state exams, and we are earning a reputation for being a high-quality school. Christians, Hindus, and Muslims all live on campus together, and we have an opportunity to reach them. Every day, the students have devotion and prayer time, and we are sharing about Jesus. They often ask us to pray for their exams and for healings as well. Children from Harvest India children's homes are now starting to attend KSK College, and they passionately share about Jesus.

One of the greatest ways we can serve children is by helping them understand education is the key that can open up hundreds of doors in their future.

Unfortunately, the longer an abandoned or orphaned child lives on the street among his or her peers – the less likely they'll want to take the path of education. We've found this to be true among a group of 25 or so young adults living near the railway in Tenali. Many have been living on the streets for years, and their daily lives consist of begging, using drugs, and jumping from train to train. When given the chance to move into one of our homes, enjoy three meals a day, and get as much education as they want, they all turned us down. Ironically, the so-called freedom they enjoy severely limits their future, and it will ultimately kill them.

This is why it is so critical for us to have enough beds available to save a child as soon as he or she is orphaned or abandoned. The quicker we can help them assimilate into a loving family environment and start enjoying the benefits of education – the better chance that child has to grow up and be the leader we need him or her to be.

Strategy #3: We prepare children to be sent out into the world.

After saving them from darkness and continuing to serve them through education, we train them up to be missionaries in our world.

Solomon writes, *"Children are a heritage from the Lord, offspring a reward from him. Like arrows in the hands of a warrior are children born in one's youth. Blessed is the man whose quiver is full of them." (Psalm 127:3-5 - NIV)*

Harvest India's quiver is full of children, and each one is being sent out into the world – launched into hospitals to care for the sick, into businesses to serve with integrity, and into remote villages to start churches where there are none.

Every single child is a gift from God, and we do everything we can to raise each one up as educated, passionate followers of Jesus.

The Bible calls them our heritage.
They are the legacy of Harvest India.

Long past my days of living on this earth, my legacy will live on in the lives of each child we helped save, serve, and send out.

You see – we raise up our children to know their life is not their own. They belong to Jesus, and He has blessed them to be a blessing. They may not have their own bedroom or a pile of toys or a closet full of clothes, but they know God has given them a second chance at life by coming to Harvest India.

Picture the trajectory of each child in this world like an arrow. Some children are launched haphazardly by their parents, while others don't even make it out of the quiver. You and I have a tremendous opportunity to aim our children in a godly direction. By raising them up in a loving environment and teaching them to follow Jesus, we're launching them with the empowerment of the Spirit – sending them farther than we ever could in our own strength.

Here's the exciting part – it's working!

Hundreds of young adults are graduating from high school, nursing school, Bible college, and the new KSK College, and we're sending them out to spread the love of Jesus throughout India.

I realize that much of this chapter focuses on what we're doing through the ministries of Harvest India, but I'm wondering how these values and strategies can be lived out in your own family. I'm curious how you can...

- Cultivate a heart of thankfulness in your child.
- Model generosity and invite your child to participate.
- Consider what type of young adult you are forming by what you are modeling as a parent.
- Help your child understand the power of their education to unlock doors in the future.
- Be more intentional about teaching your child how to follow Jesus (rather than just assuming your church will do that for you).

There's nothing like seeing a child's life transformed as they realize they are loved by God and by other human beings. Their heart begins to open, and you can see their unique personality begin to shine. The smile on their face, the glimmer in their eyes, and the laughter in their voice – it makes everything worth it.

Are you ready to help?

SMALL GROUP WEEK #10

Getting Started

1. Describe your room as a child.

2. Mahatma Gandhi once said, "A nation's greatness is measured by how it treats its weakest members." Why is this true (or not true)?

Going Deeper

3. Read Matthew 18:1-5. What is it about children that Jesus values so much, and why?

4. Re-read the three reasons why children are important to Harvest India:

   a. Children are loved and valued by God.
   b. Children will grow up and have families of their own.
   c. Children are the leaders of tomorrow.

   If we don't value, protect, and invest in children, what are the ramifications?

   If we do value them, what will be the results?

5. Read the words of Solomon in Psalm 127:3-5. How have you seen this to be true in your own family or in families around you?

Applying It To Your Life

6. Suresh shared three primary strategies that Harvest India uses to raise their children:

   a. Save children from darkness.
   b. Serve children through education.
   c. Prepare children to be sent out into the world.

   How might this same strategy apply to your own children (or children you know)?

7. After reading about Suresh's passion for children, how might you want to invest in the lives of children in your family, church, or community in a different way?

8. If children are a legacy we leave the world, what type of legacy do you want to leave?

CHAPTER 11

I AM COMPELLED TO LIVE FOR SOMETHING BEYOND MYSELF

As I look back over the years, I realize there are distinct moments that have invited me to live a compelled life.

- Almost drowning in the river and seeing my cousin carried away…dead.
- Having a tough conversation with my professor as he convinced me to stay in Bible college.
- Traveling to the West for the first time to raise support for Harvest India.
- Hearing God's voice preparing me for the death of my mother.

These are just a few moments in time when God chose to use stretching and even painful events to call me to live a new way of life. I'm reminded of the words of Joseph to his brothers, who sold him into slavery, *"You intended to harm me, but God intended it for good to accomplish what is now being done, the saving of many lives." (Genesis 50:20 – NIV)*

Whatever our enemy has meant for evil, God will turn it around for good. That's what He's done for me.

I always have the choice.
Either I allow the moment to tear me down
or follow God on the road He takes me down.

I can let it rupture my trust in Him,
or I can allow Him to shine a light on a new path.

I could have easily allowed any one of these experiences to overwhelm my faith. Instead, they became what I like to call "Compelling Moments" – moments when I'm compelled to follow Jesus wherever He leads.

Of course, my life is not perfect. This isn't how I always live, but it's how I'm choosing to live.

You don't have to wait for life to get hard in order to be compelled.
You can choose to have a Compelling Moment right now.

Sometimes, you'll feel like you have great faith.
And, other times, it will feel like you're barely holding on.
Either way, you can know that God is with you just as much in either moment.

What if you allowed today to become a Compelling Moment in your life?

My hope is that through reading of these stories you would be inspired and motivated to take action. What if you opened your heart to God and allowed Him to speak compelling words of encouragement into your spirit? What if you truly believed Jesus is worthy of your trust and that He wants to lead you down an amazing road of adventure? What if you said "yes" to what He's been calling you to do?

Here's what Compelling Moments have the power to help us do:

1. **Recognize that life is a gift from God.**

   You did not decide to come into this world. God chose you, and He created you. He saw you in your mother's womb, and He gave you the precious gift of life. He has sustained you with a beating heart and lungs filled with air for many years. What an incredible gift!

   We grow up thinking we're practically invincible and that life will last forever. The older we get – the more we realize how precious each day truly is. For me, that moment came when I lost my cousin and almost drowned.

Because God has given us this wonderful life, we must think deeply about what we're doing, about our purpose, and about how we're leveraging our time. Every day that you and I wake up is a gift from God, and we have the freedom to do whatever we wish...and the responsibility to use it wisely.

2. Clarify what's most important.

It seems like those painful experiences have a way of clarifying what's truly important, don't they? As I think back on the conversation with my professor as I considered quitting Bible school, I see how the difficulty of that moment allowed things to come into focus. What if we were able to live with more of that clarity on a daily basis?

That's what a Compelling Moment does – helps us discover what we really value in this life – and gives us the opportunity to clear away the clutter. We fill our days with extraneous "stuff" that can be enjoyable, but I often wonder if it's all that valuable.

So, what is most valuable in your life? My guess is your answers center around faith, family, and legacy. If that's the case, maybe it would be wise to ask yourself, "Does ____________________ help me build up my faith, family, or legacy?"

Fill in the blank with whatever person, job, purchase, or activity you're experiencing on a regular basis or thinking about bringing into your life. It would be smart for us to focus our energy on people, places, and things that help us live the type of life we truly want. Sure, there are plenty of things that are neutral in value (entertainment, shopping, sports, etc.), but too much investment of time or money on those things can soon become negative as well.

So, what do you value the most? How are you spending the one life you've been given in a way that supports those values?

3. Embrace your true identity.

If I were to ask you, "Who are you?" – you would probably tell me your first and last name. Although that is definitely a large part of your identity, it goes much deeper than that. Our identity is formed through the interactions with parents, teachers, coaches, and friends. We are often shaped by our experiences, by who people tell us we are, and by our own personal expectations of ourselves.

If you grew up being told that you're lazy, no good, and worthless, it's almost impossible for those words not to form part of your identity. Or, maybe you grew up in a home where love and affection were hard to find, so you started to think that something was wrong with you. Many of us live our adult lives in reaction to these negative experiences – trying to prove that we are lovable or that we are successful.

These experiences – or our reaction to them – end up forming a great deal of our identity.

Our children are passionate about serving God for the rest of their lives.

Think about the 1,300 children in Harvest India children's homes. They didn't choose to be orphaned or abandoned, but they have the opportunity to respond to their life situation. No matter what you experienced growing up or what identity you feel like you've lived with, you have the power to embrace the identity God has for you.

This is your true identity.

God created humankind to be connected in relationship with Him. By receiving His gift of grace through the death and resurrection of Jesus, you are adopted into the family of God, and you are given a brand-new name.

In The Message version, Paul writes, *"The old life is gone; a new life burgeons! Look at it! All this comes from the God who settled the relationship between us and him, and then called us to settle our relationships with each other. God put the world square with himself through the Messiah, giving the world a fresh start by offering forgiveness of sins." (2 Corinthians 5:17-19 – MSG)*

As a follower of Jesus…

You are God's son or daughter.
You are a member of God's family.
You cannot be separated from God's love.
You are forgiven.
You are free from condemnation.
You are a saint.
You are God's co-worker.
And, you can do all things through Christ who gives you strength.

When I traveled to the United States for the first time, I was confronted with a completely different way of life that included access to innumerable choices and lavish excess in comparison to what we have in India. It could have been so easy to feel 'less than' because of my culture's economic lack, but that isn't my identity. My identity is rooted in something so much deeper than the clothes I wear, the car I drive, or how much money is in my bank account.

Compelling Moments help us embrace who we *really* are – who God sees us to be. As we take on this new identity – our true identity – our attitudes, feelings, and behaviors start to come into alignment.

4. Focus on what God has called you to do.

As you're recognizing the gift of life, clarifying what's most important to you, and embracing your true identity, here are three important questions to ponder.

COMPELLED

What does God want you to do with your life?
Do you have a vision for what He wants you to accomplish?
Are you focused on His calling?

This presumes God has put you on this earth for a reason other than your own personal satisfaction. Yes, God wants you to enjoy your life. That is without question. But, I also believe He calls each one of us to do something significant as well.

James, the brother of Jesus, writes, *"Who is wise and understanding among you? Let them show it by their good life, by deeds done in the humility that comes from wisdom. But if you harbor bitter envy and selfish ambition in your hearts, do not boast about it or deny the truth. Such "wisdom" does not come down from heaven but is earthly, unspiritual, demonic. For where you have envy and selfish ambition, there you find disorder and every evil practice." (James 3:13-16 – NIV)*

James is challenging us to show that we have wisdom by living a good life filled with deeds done with an *attitude of humility*. It's not just about doing good things, but it's about doing good things for the right reason – out of love. In contrast, we are warned to avoid bitter envy and selfish ambition – which both result in "every evil practice."

The apostle Paul says, *"For we are God's handiwork, created in Christ Jesus to do good works, which God prepared in advance for us to do." (Ephesians 2:10 – NIV)*

Notice your true identity. You are "God's handiwork". Notice your calling. You were created to do good deeds. In fact, God has them prepared in advance.

That means He has a calling on your life to do something great in this world. He has given you gifts, talents, passions, and experiences to draw upon in order to live for something beyond yourself.

In The Message version, Solomon writes, *"If people can't see what God is doing, they stumble all over themselves; But when they attend to what he reveals, they are most blessed." (Proverbs 29:18 – MSG)*

TO LIVE FOR SOMETHING BEYOND MYSELF

Have you ever felt like you were stumbling all over yourself? In this very moment, ask God to give you a vision. Ask Him to help you see how He wants to use you in this unique season of life – and listen.

When my Mom passed away, I mourned and grieved her loss, but I remained focused on what God has called me to do. God used her to start the ministry, but He's using me to build on her legacy.

The reason why people talk about Mother Teresa and Billy Graham isn't because they are any more gifted or charismatic or wealthy than you are. It's because they listened to God's calling on their life, and they did something that is long lasting. They didn't choose to simply live for the short-term; they lived to leave a legacy.

Ask yourself, "Who is benefiting from my life?"

If you're willing to move outside of your normal patterns of living and trust Jesus to lead you, you can experience a Compelling Moment right now.

Are you ready to live for something beyond yourself?

I truly believe God created you for a purpose – something beyond living for the weekend, accumulating a bunch of stuff, having a fun time, and then dying. Don't you believe He put you here for a reason?

Sometimes, it takes hearing about someone else's calling to help us experience a Compelling Moment in our own life, so let me tell you what God has called *me* to do.

God has called me to be His ambassador.

When Paul calls himself "Christ's ambassador", he was not simply referring to his own calling, and he wasn't just talking about pastors or church leaders. He was calling out every single follower Jesus. We've all been given a message of reconciliation, and we are all His ambassadors.

What does an ambassador do? He or she speaks on behalf of the nation they represent. Their words and actions are a representation of the beliefs, values, and heart of that nation.

I am honored to share about God's love each and every day.

Can you believe that the God who created the entire universe trusts us to speak on His behalf? I'm humbled by the fact that He allows me to be His co-worker in this world – inviting people into relationship with Him.

As His ambassador, your life is a conduit of His love. You can speak words of wisdom into the life of people who are struggling. You have the power to bring hope to people who are desperate. God puts all His resources at your disposal as you represent Him in this world. You represent God.

<u>God has called me to serve the least, last, and lost.</u>

Several years ago, a little girl was dropped off at our campus when she was about four years old. Someone literally left her on our property and ran away. She was so scared of people and didn't want anyone to get close to her. There were scars on top of her head and body, and her thin frame was evidence she was not being fed properly.

After coaxing her into our home, she finally let us hold her and get her cleaned up. Eventually, she started playing with our daughter, Mercy, and we did everything we could to help her feel like our home was a safe place.

In her sleep, she would cry out, "Don't beat me, Jyothi. Don't beat me." As we kept reassuring her, we asked who Jyothi was, but the little girl didn't know. She told us she had been locked in a room, beaten, and made to clean things – hardly ever being fed. She didn't even know who her mother or father was. We came to find out that some neighbors heard her constant cries and eventually pulled her out of the house while the woman was gone. After being dropped off at Harvest India, it took her six to seven months to start to trust us. Four years later, she now goes to school at our campus, and she knows that she's loved.

You may have a warm, fuzzy feeling from that story, but you weren't the one holding her at 2am when she cried out in her sleep. Serving the least, last, and lost is hard work, but God gives us the strength to love some of the most broken people in this world.

There are broken and hurting people where you live, too.
They may not look like a little girl locked up in a room. Instead, they probably look like your neighbor who is struggling through a divorce, your co-worker who just got diagnosed with cancer, or your own child who is navigating the rough waters of high school.

How is God calling you to help them?

God has called me to step out from my comfort zone.

Every single one of us has a zone of comfort. It's that way of living and operating in the world we've become accustomed to. It includes where we live, what language we speak, what we eat, how we interact with others, and what we've experienced in the past.

When we do something for the first time, it's probably going to be outside our comfort zone. If it's just a little bit beyond what we're used to, it may not take much courage, but if it's really different, we may be scared to death.

Some friends in the United States thought it would be fun to take me to Disneyland since I had never been before. Roller coasters, cotton candy, and a hat with big mouse ears – way outside my comfort zone. Frankly, I have no interest in ever riding a roller coaster again, but I was willing to do it!

When it comes to the things of God, I can be just as challenged.

COMPELLED

In my early 20s, I got word from Pastor Prakash that a family wanted me to come and pray for their baby who was born with no skin. This was Nagamani's second child born with this condition; the first one died after three months. Can you imagine being in my position? What am I supposed to say to this woman? How can I pray for a miracle when things look so hopeless?

Outside my comfort zone.

As I stepped into the home, Nagamani was next to the baby – laying on banana leaves – bright red with no skin. With tears streaming down my face, I had no idea how to pray. I was questioning God, "Why do you give and then take away? God, You're the only one who can help this little baby. What are You going to do?"

I prayed with as much faith as I could muster.
Then, I went back home - discouraged.
Three days later, the baby died.

I fasted for three days, and I asked God, "Why did you take me there? You made me look like a fool. Now, who will believe me? No one will want me to pray for them."

Even though Harvest India had a church and elderly home in the area, I didn't return to Thipilakata for an entire year. I just couldn't face the pain of that experience. After 16 months, Pastor Prakash announced that Nagamani gave birth to a baby boy - with beautiful, brown skin. Many years later, she now has three healthy children who are all grown up.

There are so many questions about that experience, and they all begin with "why". Why was the baby born without skin? Why two babies in a row? Why did God take me to that place? Why didn't He heal the child? Why did Nagamani have three more healthy children?

Compelling Moments call me to trust God in the midst of the "why" while I keep living out the calling He has for me.

If I allowed these questions to consume me, I would retreat far away from anything that ever feels outside my comfort zone, and I would only allow the things that I understand to permeate the edges of my life.

TO LIVE FOR SOMETHING BEYOND MYSELF

That painful experience was over 20 years ago, but I remember it like it was yesterday. I will never know the answer to all those "whys" this side of heaven, but I do know that God continues to compel me to live outside what is easy and comfortable.

God has called me to trust Him as I venture into unknown territories to serve the broken. I have asked God to send me where others won't go - to do things others won't do.

I realize this is challenging for most people. (Trust me, it's not as though it is easy for me.) Very few people are willing to live a sacrificial life, but that is what Jesus has called me to do. In fact, He modeled that kind of life for us as He stepped down from heaven to enter our world – taking on human flesh and blood in order to share His love among us.

When Jesus says, "Follow me", He's not calling us to follow Him inside a church building on Sundays. Jesus is inviting us to travel with Him to the highways and byways of life, to love and serve those who are in need of His love.

The apostle Paul echoes this calling when he writes, *"Follow my example, as I follow the example of Christ." (1 Corinthians 11:1 – NIV)*

How much clearer can it be? If we're followers of Jesus, saved by grace, and flooded with God's love, He calls us to do what Jesus did.

Step outside our comfort zone.
Love our neighbors as we love ourselves.
Serve those who are in need – locally and globally.
Go into all the world and make disciples.

Why?

"For Christ's love compels us, because we are convinced that one died for all, and therefore all died. And he died for all, that those who live should no longer live for themselves but for him who died for them and was raised again." (2 Corinthians 5:14-15 – NIV)

I am compelled to no longer live for myself.

COMPELLED

I'm living for my God.
I'm living to save and educate thousands of orphans.
I'm living to serve widows, lepers, and the elderly.
I'm living to care for those afflicted with HIV/AIDS.
I'm living to raise up the next generation to serve Jesus Christ.
I'm living to reach every village in India with the good news of God's grace.

Today can be a Compelling Moment for you. Are you ready to live for something beyond yourself? Close your eyes and open your heart.

Ask God, "What are you compelling *me* to do in this world?"

SMALL GROUP WEEK #11

Getting Started

1. What gets you up out of bed each day?

2. What do you think it means to live for something beyond yourself?

Going Deeper

3. Read the words of Joseph to his brothers in Genesis 50:20, *"You intended to harm me, but God intended it for good to accomplish what is now being done, the saving of many lives."* How does God seem to bring good out of something painful or even evil?

4. In the beginning of this chapter, Suresh reminds us of four Compelling Moments in his life, and he then points out how that experience impacted him:

   a. Drowning resulted in recognizing that life is a gift from God.
   b. Tempted to quit school resulted in clarifying what's important.
   c. Travel to the US resulted in embracing his true identity.
   d. Death of his mother resulted in focusing on God's calling.

   Look back over those sections (and Scriptures) in this chapter and answer the question, "Which one of these lessons do you need to embrace in your own life?"

5. Take a moment and think about Compelling Moments in your own past. What happened and what did you learn?

Applying It To Your Life

6. Suresh shared what God has called him to do with his life. After reading this book, what do you sense God is compelling you to do?

7. What would it look like to take a practical next step?

8. Who would you like to invite to walk alongside you in that journey?

Thank you to all the partners of Harvest India.

ACKNOWLEDGMENTS

My wife, Heny Christina, who spent many hours by my side helping me write and name this book.

My children David, Mercy, and Nancy, who encouraged me, prayed for me, and loved me throughout the writing process.

Heather and Craig Motichko, Anita Barry, Mike Kenyon, and Brian Wurzell, who have all been faithful in supporting my dream to write a book.

Jeff Gokee, who made many contributions and suggestions along the way.

David Trotter, who helped make this dream a reality.

Many of my friends have been asking me to write a book for many years, and I thank God for all of the people who have been supporting, praying, and loving the ministry of Harvest India.

Harvest India is an Indian-based NGO [non-government organization] that seeks to serve the lowest of the low, often referred to as the Dalit people of India, through meeting real tangible needs while sharing the love of Christ.

We believe that indigenous people helping one another is the way to sustainable change for the future of India. We do however, partner with our friends in the USA, UK, Europe, and Canada to help meet the tremendous needs we encounter on a daily basis and seek to meet.

Our Mission:

To carry Christ's compassion to every village in India

We do this through four key areas of focus:

Mercy Ministries

Orphan Care

Education

Sharing the Gospel

To make a tax-deductible donation or sponsor a child:

www.harvestindia.org

Three Ways to Support Harvest India:

1. Pray that God will continue to provide us with all the resources we need to carry out our vision.

2. Give toward our mission by making a tax-deductible donation or sponsoring a child at www.harvestindia.org.

3. Serve alongside us.
Contact us for more information.

Harvest India USA
P.O. Box 10186
Costa Mesa, CA 92627

Phone: 949.701.9296
Email: info@harvestindia.org

Harvest India UK
C/O 195 Powerscourt Road
North End, Portsmouth PO2 7JH

Phone: +44 (0) 785 299 4586
Email: ukinfo@harvestindia.org

Made in the USA
Charleston, SC
15 September 2014